SIBLING RIVALRY

Seven Simple Solutions

www.**rbooks**.co.uk

Also by Karen Doherty & Georgia Coleridge

Seven Secrets of Successful Parenting

For more information on the authors and their work, see their
website at www.KarenAndGeorgia.com

SIBLING RIVALRY
Seven Simple Solutions

Karen Doherty & Georgia Coleridge

BANTAM PRESS

LONDON • TORONTO • SYDNEY • AUCKLAND • JOHANNESBURG

TRANSWORLD PUBLISHERS
61–63 Uxbridge Road, London W5 5SA
A Random House Group Company
www.rbooks.co.uk

First published in Great Britain
in 2010 by Bantam Press
an imprint of Transworld Publishers

This book is a work of non-fiction. In cases, names of people or the detail of events have been
changed to protect the privacy of others. The authors have stated to the publishers that, except
in such minor respects not affecting the substantial accuracy of the work, the contents of this
book are true.

A CIP catalogue record for this book
is available from the British Library.

ISBN 9780593059166

Addresses for Random House Group Ltd companies outside the UK
can be found at: www.randomhouse.co.uk
The Random House Group Ltd Reg. No. 954009

The Random House Group Limited supports the Forest Stewardship
Council (FSC), the leading international forest-certification organization. All our
titles that are printed on Greenpeace-approved FSC-certified paper carry the FSC logo.
Our paper procurement policy can be found at
www.rbooks.co.uk/environment

Typeset in 10/13pt Optima by Falcon Oast Graphic Art Ltd.
Printed and bound in Great Britain by Clays Ltd, Bungay, Suffolk

2 4 6 8 10 9 7 5 3 1

Mixed Sources
Product group from well-managed
forests and other controlled sources
www.fsc.org   Cert no. TT-COC-2139
© 1996 Forest Stewardship Council

With love

To my sister, Laura, and to my brother, Jon.
K.D.

To my sisters, Becky, Luisa and Portia, and to my brother, Daniel.
G.C.

Contents

Introduction

We hate it when our children don't get along. The pointless, unnecessary, infuriating, low-level bickering can go on and on.

> *'He kicked me' . . . 'She started it.'*
> *'She snatched it' . . . 'It's mine!'*
> *'He got a bigger piece' . . . 'It's not fair.'*

Between the two of us we've had to deal with all sorts of sibling issues. For a start, we have eight children between us – Karen has three girls and a boy and Georgia has three boys and a girl. As we're also siblings ourselves, we know how complicated the relationships can be. Karen is the middle child, with an older brother and a younger sister, and Georgia is the oldest in an extended family of five children.

After writing our first book, *Seven Secrets of Successful Parenting*, we didn't turn into perfect parents (as our children keep reminding us), but we did feel a lot more confident. If there was a problem with homework, bedtime or mealtimes, we could usually handle it. But dealing with sibling rivalry was altogether different, and some days when our children fought we felt we couldn't get anything right.

Clearly we weren't the only ones struggling. Sibling rivalry goes back to the beginnings of time (think Cain and Abel), and everywhere we went people kept asking us for advice and telling us hair-raising stories about what their children were up to. We found it astonishing, though somewhat reassuring, that even nice children with kind parents can be horrible to their brothers and sisters. They know each other's weak spots and go right for them.

> *My daughter has dark hair and her brother teases her about it, calling her 'moustacho' and 'mono-brow'. Unfortunately for him he's dyslexic, so she gets her own back: 'Well you're so stupid you can't even read.'*

Some parents are at their wits' end because their children find every possible opportunity to wind each other up.

> *My children can fight about anything. Even driving them to school in the morning is a nightmare. They argue over the window seats and the music. They shriek and grumble and put their feet on each other. I'm shattered before I even get to work.*

Many admit that they overreact when their children won't stop arguing. They say it's almost impossible not to snap when the petty bickering, name-calling and nastiness get to them.

> *When my children fall out I try to be reasonable, but I can only take a certain amount of it before I turn into a roaring maniac.*

At the other end of the spectrum, some parents say they don't know what to do when their children argue, so they do nothing. But they worry that they should be intervening and feel guilty when the fighting escalates.

Others say they're anxious not because their children argue, but because they hardly interact at all.

> *Maybe I was naïve because I always assumed my children would be friends. But a typical evening in our house is one boy texting his friends, another hunched over his Gameboy, and the third on Facebook attached to his iPod. They do watch* Top Gear *together, but I can't believe that counts as quality family time.*

Children also have plenty to say. They're indignant about the way their siblings get on their nerves and confess that they lash out at them in ways they'd never treat their friends.

My younger brother drives me crazy. He might do something small, but annoying. Like slurping. I can't stand it! Then I have to hit him to get him to stop. And if he won't get off the computer, I have to push him off the chair. If I just ask him nicely, he'll never let me have a go.

People told us about their children's relationships, but many were even keener to talk about their own siblings. We were surprised how often adults have complicated, unresolved feelings. Considering sibling relationships are often the longest in their lives, it's amazing how so many people are ambivalent about them.

I'm ashamed to tell you, but I don't like my brother much. We pretend to get on for my parents' sake, but when I see him I can feel my hackles rise. I'm on guard for his little put-downs, his 'helpful' advice. I'm not my normal self when he's around.

We also heard some heartbreaking stories of siblings whose lives have been shaped by their traumatic relationship. The hurt can be very deep, especially if the parents were never aware of what was going on.

My oldest sister bullied me for years, and somehow she always got away with it. She turned everything round to put herself in a good light and my parents believed her.

If my mother put her in charge of combing my hair, she'd deliberately tie it in knots first, and then yank out great chunks. When I started crying, she'd convince my mother I was lying.

She once held me down in a swimming pool until I thought I was going to drown. She told my mother she was trying to save me. This sort of thing went on until she left home.

Goodness knows what stories she spun to my father. On his deathbed he begged me to look after her. Look after her? After the misery she put me through?

While many adults are angry that their sibling got away with bullying, others resent that their sibling was spoilt or given special treatment.

> *My parents were always trying to boost my sister up. If she got only one C grade on her school report, we had a special dinner for her. But when I came home with straight As, no one mentioned it in case it upset her. When I asked why I didn't get a special dinner, my mother said that she expected me to get good grades.*

Others were jealous because another child was the obvious favourite. But instead of being upset at their parents, animosity built up between the siblings.

> *My parents have always adored my brother and they show it. They talk about him all the time and there are photographs of him everywhere. I shouldn't care, but I do. It makes me hate him.*

Some adults never grow out of their old patterns. They can irritate each other, then clash or freeze each other out until the day they die. As one sixty-five-year-old grandfather told us:

> *My sister is infuriating. Always has been. So when she asks me a question, I fend her off. Whatever topic she brings up, I yawn, look bored and say, 'Oh really, I never thought about it.' Ha! It drives her mad.*

But despite hundreds of complicated sibling stories, we also found there's plenty of genuine affection out there. Even though their children argue, lots of parents said they're also very fond of each other.

> *Sure, my girls fight – terribly. But they also refuse to go anywhere without each other.*

> *My older son calls his younger brother an ugly sausage face and wrestles him to the ground. But the little one adores it. The high point of his day is collecting his big brother from school. His whole face lights up when Bill comes out.*

Many adult siblings also told us that they had become good friends, often despite their upbringing.

> *We talk every night on the telephone and never stop laughing. She's brilliant and I love her to bits. But we didn't get on as girls. If we argued, my mother would bang our heads together – literally. We had pigtails in those days, and she'd grab them and thwack us together to 'knock some sense into us'.*
>
> *My sister was four years younger and I always had to mind her. I used to grumble and complain about it; I didn't want this little kid hanging around with me and my friends, but my mother insisted. It's a miracle we grew up to like each other.*

You might be lucky: your children might just grow up to like each other too. But if you don't want to leave it to chance, how can you encourage them to get on better and become friends? We were determined to find out.

As well as asking questions everywhere, we read dozens of books and interviewed teachers, counsellors, doctors and psychologists. Some of the professionals had strong views.

> *Leave your children to it. Or tell them to go and fight somewhere else. They'll soon work something out.*

But to us, ignoring fighting siblings seemed like a risky strategy. What if they really needed help? Other professionals were adamant that parents should get involved.

> *You've got to do something about it. It's no good sticking your head in the sand and assuming everything's fine. Siblings can terrorize each other for years, causing real emotional trauma.*

We knew how much parents wanted to put a stop to the fighting and help their children get on better, but what were they actually supposed to do? The more people we talk to, the more we realized that there is no one right answer; different things work in different families.

Whatever's going on between your children, we've found **seven** simple solutions that will make a big difference. Some of them will resonate with you immediately and you might find you're using them already. Others might be new to you. We'll show you how to use all seven in various combinations to maintain harmony. They will help you to:

- *Make each child feel loved so they aren't so competitive*
- *Tackle the causes of jealousy and resentment*
- *Put an end to bickering and resolve fights*
- *Sort out trouble spots so they don't keep happening*
- *Build a happier relationship between your children*

We're realistic enough to know that your children won't always agree about everything. But this book can help you transform your relationship with your children and their relationship with each other for the better.

We'll start by helping you to identify your parenting style and find out what you are already good at. Then we'll show you how the seven approaches will resolve even difficult sibling issues.

As Karen has so many girls and Georgia has so many boys, we've alternated between 'he' and 'she' from chapter to chapter. We've focused on children from babies to teenagers, but many of the ideas in this book work for adults too. It's never too late to resolve difficult sibling relationships and we'd love to know how you get on. Do contact us at KarenAndGeorgia.com.

Karen Doherty and Georgia Coleridge, London 2010

1

The Seven Parent Types

What Type of Parent Are You?

At the heart of this book are seven parent types, each with a different solution to sibling rivalry. They're actually based on seven important communications skills that **really work**. We've given them each a name and an illustration so they're very easy to understand and remember.

First we'll explain each parent type, then we'll show you their secrets. Read through all seven of them and see which ones you identify with most. You'll probably find you're a combination of at least two or three of them so you'll be able to work out where your strengths lie.

The Pause Parent

Pause Parents somehow manage to stay calm when their children aren't getting on, even if they're hurling abuse at each other. This is quite a feat, because sibling squabbles drive most parents crazy. The noise is exasperating and there's always the worry that they might really hurt each other.

Instinctively, most parents intervene when there's an argument. But **Pause Parents** know that if you dive straight in, you can in-advertently make things worse. You might take sides where you shouldn't, say horrible things you don't mean or mete out punishments you regret later. By keeping calm, **Pause Parents** give themselves a chance to think through what's going wrong and the best way to solve it.

We're not talking about disasters here. If someone is being tormented to the point of tears or given a black eye, of course **Pause Parents** would break it up immediately. But they try not to let low-level, everyday bickering get to them. They know how effective it can be to stay quiet and sort it out later when everyone is feeling more rational.

Even natural **Pause Parents** can sometimes find it difficult not to interfere when their children fight. But by zipping their lip and saying nothing, they often get amazing results.

The Cheerleader Parent

Cheerleader Parents are great at fostering good relationships between siblings by being positive. They notice when their children are kind or thoughtful towards each other and try to ignore it when they aren't. Like **Pause Parents**, they resist the urge to get involved every time their children bicker and they give them lots of positive attention the minute they start being more friendly. This encourages siblings to treat each other nicely and reinforces the bonds between them.

Cheerleader Parents use lots of specific praise to make each child feel appreciated and special for who they are. They know that when their children feel good about themselves, they're less likely to be competitive.

They also try very hard not to label or compare their children with phrases like, 'He's my well-behaved one,' or 'She's always naughty.' They realize that each child has a good side and a bad side, and that it's natural for them to show both at different times.

The Tuned-In Parent

Tuned-In Parents know that conflicting emotions are often the root cause of sibling arguments. They're brilliant at helping children process the feelings behind jealousy, meanness, attention-seeking or whatever it is that's making them turn against each other. Once they acknowledge the feelings behind bad behaviour, they know better behaviour often follows.

So when their children argue, **Tuned-In Parents** try listening to each one of them in turn. Once children feel understood, they're more likely to stop fighting. Even better, they may begin to understand the other's point of view, which will help them build a better relationship in the long term.

The Physical Parent

Physical Parents know that when their children feel well, they're more likely to get on with each other. They're more tolerant and less irritable if they have regular exercise, good food and enough sleep.

So instead of looking for deep psychological reasons for rivalry, **Physical Parents** keep them off junk food, shoo them out of the house to play and get them to bed on time. They find that this can stop frustration and resentments from building up. These parents are also good at being affectionate and showing each child individually how much they're loved.

The Sorted Parent

Sorted Parents are forward thinkers. They're great at anticipating trouble between siblings and avert disasters by setting up clear expectations and boundaries. They know it's much easier to head off problems beforehand, rather than trying to untangle them when everyone's already wound up. This tactic is particularly useful in big families because of the potential for convoluted disagreements. Putting in the groundwork ahead of time gives them a better chance of being heard and boosts their authority.

When an argument does blow up unexpectedly, they don't get disheartened. They know they can think through what happened and work out how to prevent it next time.

Sorted Parents are also good at teaching their children how to handle frustrations. You may not be able to prevent them from annoying each other, but you can talk through better ways of expressing themselves than snatching, kicking or calling each other names.

The Commando Parent

Commando Parents have natural authority and they're very good at being in charge. Instead of pleading or nagging their children to stop fighting, they are clear and direct about what behaviour is acceptable and what will happen if they step out of line.

These parents make it very obvious where the boundaries lie and don't allow niggly disagreements to escalate into something worse. They realize they can't force children to like each other, but they don't let their children get away with swearing, thumping, or destroying each other's stuff.

When trouble does flare up, **Commando Parents** are very good at containing it quickly. They aren't shy about stepping in and they'll certainly enforce consequences if they have to. It can be hard to gain this kind of authority, especially if sibling rivalry is already deep-rooted. But it is possible, and **Commando Parents** know how to make it happen.

The Laid-Back Parent

Laid-Back Parents are good at encouraging their children to do things for themselves. They don't feel they have to watch them every minute of the day and solve every one of their problems. They trust that, more often than not, their children will treat each other well and can work through minor disagreements on their own.

Laid-Back Parents know that a certain amount of fighting is not only inevitable, but beneficial. Learning to share, negotiate, handle arguments and cope with jealousy are important parts of growing up, so they feel that if they stepped in every time to arbitrate, they'd be doing their children a disservice. They're also happy when their children spend lots of time playing together on their own because they know how good it is for their relationship.

These parents aren't neglectful: they wouldn't hold back if someone was getting hurt. But most minor bickering doesn't get to them, because they trust that their children are fine and can sort things out for themselves.

How to Make Them Work for You

By now you may have an idea of how you're inclined to handle sibling rivalry. Sometimes it's obvious what to do when your children aren't getting on. But on those days when nothing seems to work, you may need more ideas and ammunition. So we'll talk you through each of the seven approaches in more detail.

The Secret of Pause Parents

Pause Parents stay quiet when all hell breaks loose. They don't jump in and make a bad situation worse.

Zip your lip

If you're the type who gets sucked into all your children's little squabbles, next time they start, try your hardest not to react. If you stay quiet and listen, you may find they'll stop bickering on their own, especially if they were doing it to get your attention.

When my two boys fought I'd plead and threaten all day to try and make them stop. But when I left them with someone else, they could play together without a single cross word. I finally realized why – they were fighting for my benefit!

As long as they aren't actually hurting each other, it's often more effective to stay calm and do nothing for a moment than to jump in, overreact and say things you wish you hadn't.

Calm down fast

However much you love your children, being a parent can be hard on your nerves. Even **Pause Parents** can't stay relaxed all the time, but if they get stressed, they know what to do to regain their equilibrium. They might walk out of the room, take some deep breaths or count to fifty.

When you find your children's arguing is sending your blood pressure soaring, do whatever it takes to stay calm, because if you get wound up too, you're not helping. If you can stay composed, your children's behaviour probably won't get any worse, you'll be able to regain control more easily and you won't have to spend all day feeling shaky from the stress.

Wait until later

When tempers are hot and emotions run high, it's impossible for children to behave rationally. It can also be difficult for you to work out what's going on and who, if anyone, is to blame. Though you might want to sort things out immediately, try being a **Pause Parent**. Send your children off to calm down separately and discuss the problem later, when everyone is feeling more reasonable. Whether it takes five minutes, twenty minutes or until bedtime, you'll find it's a lot easier.

❛ *When we went strawberry picking, my daughter tripped and knocked over her brother's basket. He pushed her, she fell down, squashing the fruit, and her basket tipped over too. It was carnage. She was wailing and there were mashed strawberries everywhere.*

We decided the only thing we could do was separate them. My partner and I quietly scooped up one child each and took them to the farm shop for an ice-cream, which we ate at opposite ends of the car

*park. After about fifteen minutes, they had both calmed down enough
to apologize.* 9

Keep things in perspective

If you can't stop your children fighting, it's easy to feel you're a useless parent, especially if you'd always hoped they'd get on. But **Pause Parents** don't get disheartened: they know that a certain amount of friction between siblings is inevitable. According to *Toddler Taming*, written by paediatrician Dr Christopher Green, 92 per cent of four-year-olds fight or quarrel, and from our experience it doesn't end there. So if your children argue, they're probably completely normal and you don't need to keep wondering where you went wrong.

Other parents worry that unless they can put an end to the animosity, their children are going to be scarred emotionally or hate each other for life. Again, it's important to keep this one in perspective. There's a lot you can do to help them get on better and we'll show you all sorts of great strategies in this book. So try being a **Pause Parent** and take the long view. If you can stay calm and collected, and trust that you'll find the solution, you're far less likely to overreact in the middle of an argument. This way your children won't have to deal with your stress as well as their own.

Expect to get wound up

One of the reasons we get sucked into our children's rows is that they often take us by surprise. When we're tired, stressed or racing against a deadline, pointless sibling bickering can seem a hundred times more annoying. **Pause Parents** can't anticipate everything, but if you can guess beforehand that something is going to irritate you, it can help if you mentally prepare yourself and give your children a bit of warning.

6 *By six o'cock I'm tired and past my best. If my children needle each*

other, it annoys me more than at any other time. I can't laugh it off. Once I'd worked that out, I didn't overreact every time it happened.

The Secret of Cheerleader Parents

Cheerleader Parents are positive. They notice when their children get on well and know how to praise them without making comparisons.

Notice the good, ignore the bad

Cheerleader Parents have worked out that children want our attention and prefer negative attention to no attention at all. There's a pay-off for bugging brothers and sisters if your parents notice what you're doing and get involved. When your children intentionally start annoying each other to get you to react, it can drive you right up the wall. So instead, try highlighting the behaviour you want to encourage.

The more you swap negative attention for positive, the more their behaviour will improve. **Cheerleader Parents** give a constant drip-feed of positive comments, confirming to their children over and over again that they are good people and good siblings.

Be specific

If your children have been fighting and you launch in and start gushing on about how amazingly well they get along and how wonderfully well behaved they are, they simply won't believe you. So back it up with real evidence:

- *'It was very nice of you to share your sweets.'*
- *'I noticed you let John have a turn on the swing. Thank you for that.'*
- *'It was kind of you to leave the last potato for your sister.'*

If you stick to specifics, they'll know you're telling the truth.

Don't worry about praising one child so his sibling overhears it: you can almost certainly find something nice to say about each of them.

Praise on the spot

One of the best ways to encourage your children not to fight is to catch them when they're actually being kind to each other. Even if it's the first time in a year, seize the moment and comment on it, so they'll know you've noticed:

- *'Thanks for bringing in your sister's schoolbag.'*
- *'Sounds like you're both enjoying that game!'*

If you keep encouraging them, over time they'll begin to see themselves as siblings who can and do get on, and this can help their relationship change for the better.

If there have been a lot of arguments or you have a child who feels embarrassed by compliments, praising her out loud might not work. Instead, try giving her a thumbs-up, a nod or a smile to show that you're pleased.

Be positive

Cheerleader Parents know that saying something positive can instantly change the atmosphere. Instead of making matters worse, it can tip the balance in the right direction.

So instead of:

- *'For God's sake don't start! I can't face another argument,'*

try reminding them of a time they settled their own dispute:

- *'I bet the two of you can settle this one by talking it through. Do you remember how well you sorted out that problem with the scooter?'*

Be open-minded

Even if your child is perfectly wonderful, doing fine at school and well behaved in general, if she's being horrible to her siblings it can be hard to appreciate her good points. If she has been foul to them, you might feel deep down that you can't trust her to do the right thing. So when fights break out, you tend to blame her more than the others.

Cheerleader Parents, on the other hand, are open-minded. They realize every child matures differently, each has her own strengths and weaknesses and changes over time. So they try not to label one child as the naughty or bad one.

If you tell her she's stubborn, selfish or a bully, she can start thinking of herself that way. This can make it a lot harder for her to change. True, she may go through phases of being less kind to her siblings, but if you don't label her, she may not consider it to be a defining part of her character.

Cheerleader Parents take it one step further. Though they praise their children, they try to do it without referring to a sibling, because they know that this leads to comparisons. If you call one child helpful, that's fine. But if you tell her she's 'the helpful one', it implies that another child isn't pulling her weight. If you call one child 'the sporty one', it immediately implies that the other isn't as talented. She might be quite coordinated and active, but if the title is given away to her sibling, she may feel she can't compete and so give up trying.

Not labelling one child also leaves possibilities open for the others. There's no reason why more than one of your children can't be a good netball player or singer, and it's better to allow each child to develop at her own pace.

If you want to say something nice, be specific and leave your other child's achievements out of it.

So instead of:

- *'You're getting almost as good as your sister at the recorder. And her teacher says she's a natural.'*

try:

- 'That sounds great. It's nice to hear you play.'

Instead of:

- 'Lisa's good at maths, but you're good at writing stories,'

try:

- 'I liked your story about the creepy castle, especially the bit about the skeleton.'

For a more detailed discussion on labelling children, see pages 112–16.

The Secret of Tuned-In Parents

Tuned-In Parents are good at understanding feelings. So when their children do something awful to each other, they start by listening.

Listen to their feelings

One of the most brilliant ways to end a fight is to let your children know you've heard their side. You may not even need to untangle who was right and wrong; once they feel understood, they'll often surprise you and drop the topic altogether.

❛ My boys both came running to me the other day, screaming and crying about what the other had done.
　　'Mummy – he hit me.'
　　'He kicked me. And he called me names. And he tore my shirt.'
　　They started shouting louder over each other, trying to get my attention. It all seemed incredibly complicated. Anything I heard, I repeated to try to make sure I understood what had happened.
　　'He hit you.'
　　'He kicked you and you're angry because he tore your shirt.'

'He was bugging you and that irritated you, but you didn't mean to tear it.'

I carried on like this until they finished. Then they looked at each other and apologized. ❩

Not all children are so forthcoming, however, and it's not always clear what's going on. Instead, there may be an atmosphere of simmering resentment – dirty looks, snide remarks, one child holding back tears. If you try tuning in to them individually, it may help break the deadlock and stop everything flaring up again.

Start by making a guess about how your child feels:

• *'You look pretty angry.'*

It helps to start with general statements rather than direct questions. Ironically, this is more likely to encourage her to talk:

• *'I think something must have happened upstairs.'*

If you can sound casual, she might tell you:

• *'He called me an ugly warthog just because I knocked into his stupid homework.'*

When she begins to open up, you can encourage her to keep talking:

• *'So it was an accident, and now you're upset with him for calling you names.'*

Keep listening and confirming you understand because this will help her resolve her feelings.

Accept difficult feelings

Tuned-In Parents assume that if their children do something awful to each other, there must be a reason, but they know that it's not always easy to listen calmly. You may be outraged because your child has hit her younger sister. But if you tell her off or punish her before listening to her side of the story, her bad feelings will still be there. She'll still be angry with her sister and she'll resent you too. She might even hit her again to spite you both.

Instead, listen to what she has to say without contradicting her. By tuning in you can help her work through her difficult feelings so they can start to dissipate. But this can be one of the hardest things you have to do.

Hearing one child say how much she despises the other can be absolute torture. It goes against all your instincts as a parent, especially if the child being slandered is the one you feel you need to protect. If you've never tried it before, the first time you let your child rant and rave about her sibling can be so overwhelming it may even make you feel ill.

> *I went to parenting classes because my daughter was so foul to her younger brother. I did everything I could to get her to stop, but nothing worked. The teacher suggested that next time she started to complain about him, I should just listen and let her speak.*
>
> *Well I did it, but it was horrible. All sorts of vile things came out of her mouth. 'I hate him. I wish he was dead. Why was he born? You should just get rid of him!'*
>
> *Staying quiet while she carried on like this felt all wrong. I was terrified of letting her say all this awful stuff. Maybe she'd get more worked up and do something terrible to him. I've never felt such fear.*
>
> *But I trusted the teacher, so I kept quiet. After ten minutes she blew herself out and came and sat on my lap. I was really surprised because after that she was a lot, and I mean a LOT, nicer to him.*
>
> *Their relationship still isn't perfect, but if either of them complains to me about the other now, it's not such an ordeal to listen.*

If your child's feelings have been building up for a while, they may get more intense before they diminish and you may be quite shocked by what she says. But keep tuning in. You're letting the steam out of an emotional pressure cooker. Once you do, her feelings won't seem so overwhelming. She'll be able to cope with them better, and so will you.

Imagine it could happen

A wonderful way to show your child that you take her feelings seriously is to use a bit of humour. If she complains that you spend too much time with the baby, take her wishes to the fantastic extreme and imagine what could happen. You could give her a hug and say:

- *'Wouldn't it be amazing if Dad could look after her all day and night? Then you and I could play games and eat ice-cream together whenever we wanted.'*

If you've never tried anything like this before, you might worry that she'll take what you say literally. But if you make the fantasy preposterous enough, she'll know it isn't really going to happen. This isn't about fobbing your child off with a joke, but showing her that you know how strongly she feels. You might be amazed to find that this is exactly what she needs.

This technique can also work well for older children. If you're feeling confident and can keep your tone light, you might find that you can dissipate a lot of their anger by repeating back what they say, but exaggerating it. You could try:

- *'I can tell you're FURIOUS he broke the Xbox. I bet you want to hang your brother upside down and dip him in boiling oil!'*

Again, your child knows it's not going to happen, but it may just be enough to calm her down.

Respect their feelings

Tuned-In Parents know that it's unkind and divisive when parents say bad things about one sibling to the other. Even if one child has been aggressive, **Tuned-In Parents** wouldn't refer to her as the bad one or a bully. They know that if she overhears she'll probably feel more resentful and angry.

Your aggressive child already knows she shouldn't have hit her sister, called her names, poked her, irritated her or whatever, so why rub it in? Her behaviour or reactions may have been wrong, but she isn't a bad person. She's simply a child who has made a mistake, and she probably felt justified at the time.

So instead of saying to the child who's been hurt:

- *'I'm so sick of your sister being mean. She's such a pain,'*

try staying neutral and listen:

- *'I see. She kicked you because you knocked over her iPod. And you tried to apologize.'*

Rather than blaming, **Tuned-In Parents** try to understand both sides of the story. If one child did something heinous, you don't have to agree that she did the right thing; just acknowledge her view of what happened and why:

- *'So she was jumping around the room again, even though you've asked her a million times not to. And then she tripped over your iPod cable.'*

It's astonishing how often both children are to blame.

Even if it's in private, it's corrosive to criticize a child to a sibling because they have a way of throwing the things you've said back in each other's faces.

If you confide in one, she might feel good about being favoured by being given privileged information that boosts her up while putting the other one down. But on other levels, it can be very uncomfortable. Deep down she may feel guilty for colluding against him. She may also worry that if you criticize him, you may do the same to her. This can create an unpleasant dynamic, where she'll do anything to make him seem to be the bad guy so that she remains your favourite.

You can also inadvertently set up a nasty precedent of going on about each other's faults, which can easily last your children's life-time. Everyone will be far happier if you can help your children to be on the same side.

Reconnect

Even **Tuned-In Parents** get it wrong. Like the rest of us, they over-react, say the wrong thing or hand out unfair punishments. But they're not afraid to admit it. They know how important it is to say sorry and reconnect with their children. It gives them a chance to let go of the guilt and start again.

Some parents feel they shouldn't apologize to their children because it's a sign of weakness. But reconnecting isn't grovelling: it's keeping the lines of communication open. If your children deserved time out for pulling each other's hair, you don't need to beg their forgiveness for sending them to their rooms. But if you bellowed at the top of your voice and dragged them there, you can say how very much you regret it.

Reconnecting sets a very good example to your children. If they can also get into the habit of apologizing, it's one of the easiest and quickest ways to become friends again after an argument.

The Secret of Physical Parents

Physical Parents know that if their children feel well, they're more likely to get on.

Get them moving

Children often squabble if they sit around all day in front of the television or computer, and getting them out of the house can work miracles. Then the aggro has a chance to evaporate instead of bouncing off the walls of the living room. If it's a rainy day and you can't get outside, play-fighting, wrestling or chucking pillows around are great ways for your children to work off some energy. If they're rolling around scrapping like bear cubs, don't always assume that they're about to kill each other; as long as they're both having fun, it's fine.

Feed them well

Physical Parents know that a snack can work wonders for family morale. If they have low blood sugar, some children can be whiney, others grumpy or downright mean.

> *One of my children was particularly awful every afternoon. Nothing was ever right for him. He couldn't stand his brother humming and he'd cry if his sister teased him. It took a while to figure it out, but he copes much better if I give him a snack as soon as he gets out of school.*

Physical parents aim for healthy food and steer clear of too much sugar.

> *I try not to let my son eat too much rubbish because it makes him hyperactive and hypersensitive.*

Get them to bed

Exhausted children can mean fractious, stroppy children who pick fights and won't listen to reason. So **Physical Parents** try to get them to bed at a reasonable hour. That way everyone has enough time to relax and go to sleep. On days when it's all going horribly wrong, the answer is often to get them to bed as early as possible and cross your fingers that they'll be less bolshie in the morning.

If you have a toddler who's causing havoc, she's likely to be in a better mood after a nap. Another bonus is that while she's sleeping, there's the chance for you to spend time with your other children.

Be affectionate

Lots of siblings fight because they're jealous and suspect that there isn't enough of your love to go round. You can tell them a hundred times that they're gorgeous and special, but if they feel insecure, you may not be able to convince them. **Physical Parents** know that hugs and kisses can show them how much they are loved on a deeper level than words.

Other children may fight to get your attention. But if you continually give them lots of affection, the need won't be so great. Sitting with your arm round them makes them feel safe and reassures them that you care. If they're reluctant to let you hug them (maybe they think it's sissy or that they've grown out of it), try sitting next to them to watch television, lying on their bed to read a story, kissing them on top of their head, massaging their feet or having a mock wrestling match. Even if your child doesn't like much affection, there are all sorts of ways of making contact without being soppy about it.

Just be there

Many parents find their children fight most when they haven't been able to spend much time with them.

When I went to America for a week, my children started acting up the minute I arrived home. My daughter was playing the piano and my son started pounding the low notes to drown her out. Then when he set up his Playmobil men, she flicked them all over. It was awful! They're not normally like that. But then normally I don't go away for so long.

The fighting can become acute when one parent is no longer always there.

When my partner and I separated, my children started scrapping a lot. They are really upset about their dad, but they take it out on me and each other.

It's not easy balancing parenthood with jobs, mortgages and a thousand claims on our time. Even full-time parents can't roll play dough with their children all day, however much they'd like to. Most of us have to run around simply to stay in the same place and keep chaos at bay. But **Physical Parents** make it a priority to spend as much time as possible with their children.

The Secret of Sorted Parents

Sorted Parents are forward thinkers. They anticipate stressful family situations and prepare their children to cope with them.

Bite the bullet

Sibling arguments are a big pain in the neck. When our children aren't fighting, most of us breathe a sigh of relief, cross our fingers and hope there won't be any more trouble. But **Sorted Parents** know problems don't always magically disappear on their own. Instead of hoping their children will grow out of it one day, they carve out time to think through a strategy and make it work. Though they're as busy as the rest of us, they know that dealing with issues now can avoid months or even years of bickering and bad feelings.

Sort your systems

Sorted Parents see what's going wrong and work out a way to prevent it happening again in the future.

My children argued perpetually over the music in the car. So I decided to buy each of them an iPod for Christmas. It was worth every penny.
    It took ages to download all our CDs, but I'm glad I got it organized. Last summer we drove right through France and the journey was almost stress free.

Give advance warning

When there's a recurring problem, **Sorted Parents** know that it helps to talk it through before it happens again. For example, if one child consistently annoys her sibling and the other continually overreacts, it helps to show them what other options they have:

- *'You know your sister hates you touching her pencil case. Next time you can't find colouring pencils or sellotape, come and ask me and I'll help you.'*

- *'I can see how angry you are. But instead of calling him names or thumping him, try telling him exactly what bothers you. You could say, "When you take things out of my bag it makes me REALLY angry – especially when you don't give them back."'*

When your children fight in front of others, it can be excruciatingly embarrassing. So **Sorted Parents** tell their children how to behave long before arriving at the supermarket or at their grandparents' house. They find this works much better than hissing warnings and threats when things start going downhill.

Set up rules

When everyone is seriously wound up, it's almost impossible to jump in with a new rule and solve the problem on the spot. **Sorted Parents** know the more contentious the issue, the more groundwork they need to put in ahead of time. If children have a chance to get used to a new rule first, it's much easier to enforce.

When my daughter started violin lessons, the others kept disturbing her. When she'd practise in the main room they'd tease her, saying it sounded like the death throes of a strangled cat. She would end up in tears and refuse to play. I kept shouting at them to leave her alone, but it didn't work.

Finally I set up a new rule. I told everyone that after half-term she was going to do her practising in her bedroom with the door closed, where no one was allowed to interrupt her. I reminded everyone a couple of times what was going to happen and, to my surprise, it worked. From day one, no one disturbed her at all.

You may not like the idea of having lots of rules, but it doesn't mean you have to run your house like an army camp. You're aiming for fewer arguments, not more, by clarifying what is acceptable behaviour. By taking time to let everyone know 'This is the way things are going to be around here', you may not even need to get tough about it later.

Train them up

If your children are in the habit of being nasty to each other, sometimes it's not enough to tell them to stop. **Sorted Parents** spend time showing and explaining what they can do instead.

> When my son loses his temper, he loses it badly, hits his siblings and then gets into trouble. I suggested that perhaps he could walk away to calm down, and we talked it through quite a few times.
>
> Yesterday a stupid argument blew up. My daughter shoved his plate, and his cheese on toast fell on to the floor. I thought he was going to hurt her. But without a word he got up, walked into the bathroom and stayed there for half an hour. When he came out she apologized, cleaned it up and the rest of the evening was fine. I told him how well he'd done and I know he felt quite proud of himself.

The Secret of Commando Parents

Commando Parents have natural authority and solve family fights without nagging or shouting. They're great at setting boundaries and enforcing consequences.

Give orders that don't sound like orders

Though they can be firm, **Commando Parents** don't always go straight in with the tough stuff. Instead of barking orders, which can make quarrelling children more defiant, they might start with a suggestion that doesn't sound like an order at all. The idea is to encourage your children to want to do the right thing, rather than forcing them to obey you. **Commando Parents** might:

Give options *'I don't like you fighting in here. Do you want to argue outside or in your bedroom?'*

Say it in a word Instead of: *'I've told you a million times not to swear and call each other names, blah, blah . . .'* try: *'Language!'*

Describe what you see *'You both want the same toy.'* Once it's put into words, your children may not be so wound up about it.

Ask what comes next Instead of: *'Say sorry too. NOW!'* try: *'She's apologized. Now what do you need to do?'*

Give a quick reminder *'If you paint up at the table, the baby won't be able to reach your picture.'*

Whisper *'Could you two keep the noise down?'* Surprisingly, this is often far more effective than shouting.

Give thanks in advance *'Thanks for taking turns on the scooter.'* Say it as the first child hops on (planting the seed that he is going to have to share).

Write a note *'These brownies are for Tom's class picnic. DO NOT EAT THEM.'* When something's written down, siblings often take it seriously.

Refer to the rules *'We don't hit people.'* *'In this house we don't call names.'*

Bonus points if you set up these rules ahead of time like a **Sorted Parent**.

Give information

Instead of taking sides or threatening punishments, **Commando Parents** will often give information in a non-threatening, matter-of-fact way.

- *'This is a problem. There are two of you and only one more slice of pizza.'*

Once it's put into words, children may not feel so wound up about it because they know you understand the problem and they can see more clearly why they're fighting. This can work particularly well for explosive situations. You aren't taking sides, ordering anyone around or getting worked up. You are simply stating a fact, which can stop the problem in its tracks or prevent it escalating.

Express your feelings

Commando Parents sometimes get their children to stop bickering by telling them honestly how they feel about it:

- *'I hate it when you two fight, especially when you're shouting right in my ear.'*
- *'Hearing you talk to each other that way really upsets me. I can't stand that kind of language.'*

Expressing yourself this way is so much more effective than, 'You are nightmares. Stop it at once!'

You'll know it's working when you hear your children doing the same thing.

My daughter kept yelling at her little sister to stay away from her gerbil, but it didn't work. Then one day she explained, 'It really bugs me when you open his cage. I don't want to have to worry about you losing him when I'm at school.'

Stand your ground

When necessary, **Commando Parents** can be quite firm. But having natural authority doesn't mean shouting louder or more often. Instead, they make eye contact and show that they are not budging until their children do the right thing.

My son kept prodding his sister and trying to distract her at the table. I told him twice that she didn't like it, but he ignored me. So I went round, knelt down next to his chair and looked straight at him. 'Susy doesn't like that, and neither do I.' He rolled his eyes, but I kept quiet, and stayed where I was. Eventually he looked back at me and said he was sorry.

Amazingly, he stopped pestering her. I was so glad I didn't end up yelling at him.

With older children it can be harder, but **Commando Parents** stand their ground, refusing to plead, nag or leave until their children cut it out. Teachers and school heads are often incredibly good at this: separating misbehaving children by standing confidently with arms folded and a stern look.

Use rewards and consequences

Commando Parents know that setting consequences for their children's behaviour can be very effective. But they're careful not to threaten anything they can't enforce, and they try to make the punishment fit the crime.

- *If they're fighting over the same toy, then . . . you might take it away until they can work out a way to share it.*
- *If they're fighting over the television, then . . . you might turn it off until they can agree what to watch.*
- *If they're fighting just to aggravate you, then . . . they might have to go upstairs and fight on their own, or you'll go upstairs so that they lose their audience.*

The best reward for getting along is doing more things together that you all enjoy. A family trip to the park is better than doling out sweets, toys or money.

The Secret of Laid-Back Parents

Laid-Back Parents allow their children to develop a good relationship. They encourage them to spend time together and sort problems out themselves.

Allow them to do more

Laid-Back Parents try hard to let siblings develop a relationship of their own. They know that children often get on better when their parents aren't hovering over them.

My girls bicker constantly when they're with me in the house, and keep running to me with complaints. But when they're in their playhouse at the bottom of the garden, they entertain themselves happily. When I check on them, they're always getting on fine without me.

By allowing your children to do things on their own, they can start to build their own relationship. Once they have a little repertoire of shared experiences, they're far more likely to act like a team.

If you have very small children, you won't be able to leave them entirely on their own. But you can still encourage their relationship – with supervision, most toddlers can hold a baby on their lap, and when they're a little older they can happily make up all sorts of games together.

Ask for solutions

Laid-Back Parents encourage their children to sort out their disagreements for themselves. So when their child comes in moaning about her sibling, they won't swoop in and decide who was right and who was wrong, or dish out punishments. Instead they might ask her what she could do about it. They know their children have good ideas and that with a little prompting they can often figure things out. Furthermore, if the solution comes from them, it's more likely to work. Try:

- *'This does seem tricky. What can we do about it?'*

If you're not used to being a **Laid-Back Parent**, you might be staggered by how creative your children can be. Often they'll find a good solution that never occurred to you. If you appreciate their ideas, they'll realize they can solve problems on their own and gain confidence. Over time they'll get better at it and this skill will be very useful to them in all sorts of situations. It can also help take the strain off you because it's not always you making unpopular decisions and having to enforce them.

Ask the family for ideas

As fighting often affects the whole family, **Laid-Back Parents** might ask everyone for ideas on how to put an end to it. They'd either do it informally by talking to each child separately at bedtime, or by sitting everyone down at the table.

- *'I know you all have good ideas. How do you think you could share the plasticine?'*

Try writing down every single suggestion, even if it's silly. If you show you're taking everyone's ideas seriously, your children will probably stop footling around and come up with some reasonable solutions.

Be a role model

Laid-Back Parents realize that being a good role model can be more effective than lecturing or ordering children to be kind to each other. Of course none of us can get it right all the time, but at least we can try to catch some of our worst habits.

❝ *I realized that my two-year-old always called his older sister's name melodiously, but screeched his brother's name in an unpleasant, violent tone. It suddenly dawned on me: that's how he thought you said them because he's been listening to me!* ❞

What you do and say sets the ethos of the house. If you compliment your children, for example, you'll find they're more likely to say nice things to each other. If you stay in charge without shouting or hitting, your children are less likely to shout and hit each other.

Notice we say **more** likely and **less** likely – children can be spiteful and horrible to their siblings even if their parents do set a good example. Most children haven't learned to moderate their feelings and they can pick up all sorts of terrible words and behaviour from school and television. But if you can be a reasonably good role model, it helps.

Get help

Laid-Back Parents know that the noise, mess and stress of looking after children can get to anybody. So they don't feel guilty or feeble if they have to ask for help. They know they can't do everything on their own, so they call on their families and friends if they need them.

This is good for your own sanity as well as for sibling relationships. When the atmosphere is calm, the family dynamic changes for the better and your children are less likely to struggle for your attention and turn against each other.

These approaches work incredibly well. The more of them you can use, the easier it will be to help your children, though depending what type of parent you are, some of them will feel more natural to you than others. Next we'll look at some of the reasons your children might not be getting on.

2

Why Siblings Don't Get On

What's Going On in Your Family?

You've told your children to separate, but they're back in the same room again annoying each other. It's as though they're drawn together like magnets. Why on earth can't they just leave each other alone!

There are endless reasons why children argue and fight, and plenty more why they don't talk to each other at all. But understanding the causes of sibling rivalry isn't always easy. Often it's to do with a complicated combination of children, temperaments and circumstances in your family. We'll look at four main reasons siblings clash:

- *They're stuck with the siblings they've got*
- *They irritate each other*
- *Parents make things worse*
- *Circumstances affect their relationship*

But not all sibling rivalry is bad. We'll also look at:

- *How fighting might even be good for your children*

They're Stuck with the Siblings They've Got

Interviewing parents for this book, we found that many suspect the size or age range of their family is at the root of their problems.

Some parents worry that their children have nothing in common because they're too far apart in age.

My daughter is six years older than her sister. It's not surprising they can't build much of a relationship.

Some say their children constantly compete because there are only two of them.

My two boys fight over everything. 'He's got a bigger room'; 'He's got more toys'. I wish they'd stop comparing themselves.

Some parents are anxious because one child keeps getting left out.

I've got three children. What a terrible mistake. No matter what, it's always two against one.

Others recognize that the more children they have, the more potential there is for conflict.

My family is so huge it's hard to cope. My two children and our daughter live with us, and my three stepchildren come at weekends. It's really hard to keep the peace. The only one who likes having all eight of us in the house is our dog!

Raising children is like being dealt a hand of cards – you can only play the ones you're given. There are an almost infinite number of combinations: you may have all girls, four children in three years (yes, this happened to a friend of ours and she still looks pretty shell-shocked) or siblings thirty years apart. There's also every permutation of step-family, and every single child comes with his own personality.

Whether your children are similar, different or unequally matched, you may feel that there is nothing you can do about the family you've got. And in a way you're right: a lot of it is down to luck, and you're stuck with the individuals you've got in the order they were born. (See pages 57–9 for more thoughts on birth order.)

Unfortunately, they're also stuck with each other. When they're together so much, even little aggravations can seem huge and it's easy to forget how intense their feelings can be.

> *My sister is so annoying. She chews with her mouth open, in the mornings she has bad breath, and I can hear her BREATHING.*

You may worry that two or more of your children simply don't get on and wonder if there's anything you can do about it. Try shuffling your hand and changing the pattern. It's remarkable, for example, how siblings can interact totally differently when one child is away for the afternoon or the weekend. Treaties and boundaries get renegotiated and enemies can become friends. For some parents it can be a real relief to realize sibling relationships aren't necessarily set in stone.

> *Our daughters fight constantly over everything. But the strangest thing happens. When our son is away, they get along just fine and can play together for hours.*

If you suspect that the shape of your family is part of the problem, you might feel there's nothing you can do to improve their relationship. But we'll show you how other factors can make an even bigger difference. The more clearly you see what's going on, the easier it will be to resolve a lot of problems between your children.

They Irritate Each Other

There's no doubt about it: siblings can find each other infuriating. Though they might wind each other up on purpose, often they just can't help it. If one or more of your children seems harder to get on with than the others, it's almost certainly not intentional.

Some children are easygoing, while others are fully paid-up members of the awkward squad. But the majority go through stages of being more or less difficult. Many parents find their children take it in turns: as soon as a tricky child becomes easier to manage, another steps up to the plate.

❝ My son was always the stroppy one, but when he started school he started being nicer to his sister. Then would you believe it? She started being a pain and picking fights with him. ❞

Here are some of the reasons your children might clash. The point isn't to label them, but to try to figure out what's upsetting them or why they overreact.

They're Very Different or Too Similar

When they don't have much in common

You'd think children with the same parents, who grow up in the same house with roughly the same experiences, would share a lot of common ground. But they can be surprisingly different, and they can find their differences really annoying.

❝ My children approach the world from opposite directions. He thinks she's an airhead, she thinks he's a geek. It's just a personality clash. They've got to live together, but they certainly wouldn't choose each other as friends. ❞

When they want to be seen as individuals

Some parents have the opposite problem: their children don't get on because they have too much in common. Each one is fighting to carve out his own identity.

❝ My teenage sons have such similar tastes and interests that they argue ferociously. They both love football, so they can debate for hours about who supports the better team. If they go out shopping separately, they often come back with the same clothes (currently they are both fixated on Adidas) and they quarrel about who liked what first. It would be funny, but they both get so wound up about it. ❞

According to psychologists, we all have a side to us that we'd rather not admit to, so people who remind us of ourselves can be the most annoying. If siblings are confronted with someone who looks or sounds similar, uses similar words or has similar interests, they can hate each other for it and try to play up their differences.

My mother put my twin sister and me in matching dresses. My sister loved looking like me, but I couldn't stand it. I rebelled and kept insisting on wearing trousers.

Even when children aren't twins, they'll still want to be individuals. Part of growing up is finding out who you are in relation to others. Though some children learn by copying their older siblings, others want to stake out their own territory.

They're Sensitive or Reactive

When they're easily upset

Hypersensitive children can be difficult siblings. They may take things personally or see an insult where none was meant. When their feelings are hurt, they can drive others mad by coming across as a whinger, victim or cry-baby. And they may find it impossible to ignore even the mildest teasing.

Often, sensitive children can't tolerate change or anything that's too extreme. They may hate loud noises, raised voices or blaring music, and lash out at whoever is responsible. Or they might raise hell if anyone makes a peep when they're trying to sleep. How they feel has a direct effect on how they interact, so if a sensitive child is overtired or has eaten too much junk, you can bet he'll stir things up.

When they overreact to provocation

This kind of child gets into fights with his siblings whenever he feels slighted in any way. Every time anyone accidentally touches him, he'll immediately retaliate. When something bothers him, he gets so angry so quickly you can almost see the steam coming out of his ears.

Every time my son gets upset, he screams his head off or punches someone. It's a nightmare for his sisters.

They Love the Drama

When they get bored
So often children pick fights with each other simply because they're bored. It's a lot more fun to bug siblings than do nothing. If they haven't got anything more exciting to do than loaf around, it's no surprise if they start pestering each other.

When they push for attention
Some children butt into every conversation and muscle into every game. This often happens when a younger child is desperate to get his older siblings' attention. He may be clingy and insist on holding hands when his siblings aren't interested. Even if he knows he's being irritating, he might keep trying to get his siblings' approval.

When they find arguments irresistible
When there's trouble brewing, some children can't help getting right in the middle of it. They may have no intention of being sucked into the swirling vortex of energy, but somehow they manage to, time and again. There they are, at the epicentre of every sibling argument, whether it has anything to do with them or not.

Some may stir everything up for the sport of it, others try to be peacemakers. Whatever their reasons, they make things worse by poking their noses into other people's business, handing out advice or irritating everyone.

They Have Strong Characters

When they want to be top dog
Being competitive about their achievements goes with the territory for most siblings. When they're widely spaced, it may not be as much of an issue, but if they're close together (and particularly if the older one feels threatened), this can be a huge problem.

> *My oldest son has always been competitive. The problem is that his younger sister is very bright and was moved up into his year at school. He was outraged and has done everything he can to make her life a misery.*
>
> *The younger one fights back. She doesn't see why she should kowtow to anyone. It's been a complete disater for their relationship because he just can't accept it.*

Though some children are fighters, others back off. But they can end up feeling resentful or that they're losing out.

> *My older brother and I were both good rugger players, but he was so competitive that I stopped playing. I couldn't stand all the arguing about who played better or whose match went better.*

Children can also compete for your time and attention (see page 63).

When they enjoy the feeling of power

Some older children like bossing their younger siblings around and threaten them if they don't obey instructions. But in some families smaller children have power too – they know they can annoy the older children and get them into trouble.

They Insist on Their Rights

When they like to get their own way

Some children have strong views and won't compromise on even the tiniest, most insignificant issues. This stubborn type won't stop arguing for what he feels he deserves – the channel he wants to watch on television or the front seat of the car, whether it is his turn or not.

This can be irksome for his siblings, as obstinate children often get away with it. When you can't force them to behave, you might give up and focus, instead, on their compliant brothers and sisters. If you are tougher on them, or make them do more chores than their headstrong sibling, it's not surprising if they get resentful.

❛ Yesterday my husband told my daughter to wipe the table. 'Why do you always ask me?' she said. 'Why don't you ever ask Alfie?'

'Um, because I can't make him do it,' he said sheepishly. At least he was honest. ❜

When they have a strong sense of justice

These children can't bear it when things aren't fair. They may recall, weeks later, that someone else got the best seat on the sofa or the window seat in the car, when no one else cares or remembers anything about it.

A child like this will know exactly how old everyone was when they got their first bicycle or mobile phone and will complain bitterly if the age changes. He'll keep tabs on who does which chores and feel outraged if his sibling's bad behaviour earns a lighter punishment than his own.

When they have a strong sense of ownership

This type of child goes ballistic when someone touches his stuff, and might put 'Do not enter or you DIE' signs up on his bedroom door.

He might insist that no one else can use his birthday present, even if he no longer plays with it, and this can seem quite selfish. But for many children the issue is more subtle. It could be that having one organized place of his own, whether it's a whole bedroom or just one shelf, makes him feel secure. So he feels invaded when siblings barge into his room and fiddle with his things, and gets deeply upset when his possessions are borrowed, lost or broken.

They Don't Handle Feelings Appropriately

When they aren't sensitive to other people's feelings

Some children don't realize that their comments are hurtful. Often they fail to pick up on social cues, so don't know when enough is enough. This kind of child might make his sister cry by laughing at her painting or pouring scorn on her Beanie Baby collection. Or he might get into fights because he doesn't know when a joke crosses the line and becomes teasing, or even bullying.

You might just think this type of child has a mean streak, but lots of children don't know how to be kind and tactful until we teach them how to do it, and it takes some longer to learn than others.

When they find it hard to let go of their own feelings

Long after everybody else has apologized and made up after an argument, some children can't let grievances go. They carry on glowering and sulking far longer than necessary and, even when you think they've calmed down, their pent-up resentment is still there under the surface. So if one of their siblings teases them or unintentionally insults them, they flare up again. Though they might have had a good reason to be angry in the first place, it's not surprising if they don't get the sympathy vote from anybody.

They May Have Got into the Habit of Fighting

When they assume the worst

If your children have been going through a bad patch of needling or teasing, they can begin misinterpreting each other, viewing every action as intentionally irritating or unkind.

❛ The other day Paul was skateboarding and accidentally bumped into Lauren's legs. I was watching and saw he'd tried hard to miss her. She wasn't hurt, but she cried on and on, insisting he did it on purpose. No matter how many times he apologized, she refused to forgive him and kept wailing, 'You're always so mean to me!' ❜

Once they're expecting the worst, even subtle glances and innocent remarks can set them off.

❝ Oh for heaven's sake! Saskia came to me in tears because Freya rolled her eyes at her. I swear the only way to deal with these two is to make sure they never speak, touch or even look at each other. ❞

When they get into bad habits

Having a go at each other can become part of your children's repertoire – a habit that, like any other, is very hard to break. When they see each other they go straight into autopilot, winding each other up and reacting, over and over again. They don't think through what they do or say, as they would with their friends. Instead they fall back on their usual pattern of sniping at each other and getting worked up about it.

Parents Make Things Worse

Looking after one child is hard enough, and life becomes exponentially more complicated the more children you have. You've got to manage with less time and sleep, and more mess, noise and aggravation.

It's hard to admit, especially when we're trying so hard, but sometimes we can actually make our children's relationships worse. Most of us don't set out to favour one child or turn them against each other, but our good intentions can backfire and we can end up with the opposite of what we're aiming for. If your children don't get on as well as you'd like, it's worth considering whether you might be part of the problem.

You May Treat Your Children Differently

When you try too hard to make things fair
If you feel sorry for one child or feel he has a raw deal compared
to another, you might think it's up to you to level the playing field.

> *My husband and our middle daughter don't get along. So I spoil her
> to make up for it.*

Favouring one child can easily happen.

> *My boys are so different. David has everything going for him. He's
> smart, sporty and makes friends easily. But Ollie is shy and finds every-
> thing more difficult.*
>
> *When David brings home gold stars and sports badges, Ollie looks
> like a sad little puppy. You can see how small it makes him feel. So I
> downplay David's achievements and make a big deal of Ollie's to help
> him feel better about himself.*

Though some parents try to build one child up, others try to
make things fair by squashing the other one down.

> *When my children fight, I come down hard on my daughter. She's
> bigger and stronger and should know better. Her brother is much
> younger and needs protecting.*

You may feel you understand one child better
Lots of parents find some of their children harder to get on with
than others. You may feel you have the closest relationship with
the one who appears to need you the most.

> *My younger daughter is quite sensitive. We spend a lot of time
> together doing her homework and we talk about everything. My son,
> on the other hand, is very independent. He doesn't really need me.*

Some children just get on your nerves.

> *My son often loses his temper and I hate it. Even if he's right, he
> expresses himself in such a horrible way I find I often take my
> daughter's side.*

Personality clashes make it very hard to see your child clearly. In your own mind you might label this child as the difficult one.

My mother always said my brother and I fought because I was a very disruptive, out-of-control child. But she never worked out why I was so angry: it was because she kept telling everyone how horrible I was and indulging my little brother.

You May Not Be Handling Arguments Effectively

You may be overreacting to their disputes
Children want our attention, and one sure-fire way to get it is to start winding each other up. Once they realize how effective it is, they may intentionally provoke each other to get a rise out of us. It's nearly impossible not to get involved, especially when we hear their shrieks and wails.

When I hear my children scrapping, I try to break it up immediately. I'm afraid they're going to hurt each other.

Many parents find they keep taking the bait, getting sucked into their children's arguments over and over again. As a result, their children have good reason to carry on fighting.

You may be too soft, too strict or inconsistent
Lots of parents feel absolutely overwhelmed when their children clash and wish they knew how to make things better. However hard they try, nothing works.

Some plead ineffectually for everyone to stop. Others shout and mete out punishments that make everybody ten times angrier. Lots of parents simply don't know which way to go.

You may find it hard to set a good example
Ideally, we would all be such brilliant parents that our children would pick up by osmosis how to get on with each other. Simply

by copying us they would be able to express themselves tactfully and effectively.

Unfortunately, in reality they suck up all the things we wish we hadn't said and try them out on their siblings in that awful tone of voice we wish we hadn't used. Anything you do can filter into the way they treat each other.

❝ My parents used to smack us to get us to behave. I'm sure this is why my brothers and I used to hit each other all the time. ❞

Some parents find it so difficult to express feelings that their children also find it hard to talk to each other.

❝ When I was a child, all sorts of emotional stuff was going on, like my parents getting divorced. But they kept a stiff upper lip and tried to pretend it wasn't happening. As a result, my sisters and I could chat about small things, but never the big ones. It was all too intense.

When I get stressed with my own children, I go very quiet and pale, and sort of freeze up. I like the way my husband is so straightforward. If there's a problem, he tackles it head on. I think he sets a much better example than I do. ❞

If children don't learn from us how to get along, they'll have to learn from their friends, which is a bit of a lottery. They'll also pick it up from the TV, which is even more worrying. Unfortunately, conflict is good for ratings, so they're far more likely to see people shouting or getting revenge than resolving their differences.

Birth Order

Lots of parents treat their children differently simply because of the order in which they were born. Often they don't even realize they're being unfair, and they certainly don't anticipate the problems it can cause.

Siblings can also put themselves into roles or expect to be treated better because of their position in the family. Once the sibling dynamic gets set up, one or all of them can end up feeling resentful about it.

- **Oldest children** are often resented for being bossy and acting superior just because they were born first.

My older brother thinks he has the right to order me around. He gets a better deal on everything.

Oldest children, for their part, can feel irritated because they've had to be responsible for younger siblings and fight for the privileges the others take for granted.

My mother was always much tougher on me. She needed help around the house and someone to watch the younger children, and she expected me to do it.

- **Middle children** are often thought of as 'the difficult child', and they can be resented by their siblings for being attention-seekers. But as they aren't the oldest or the youngest, many feel they have to fight to be noticed. Lots of middle children feel hard done by because they've never had special treatment.

I'm the classic middle child. My parents thought everything my older brother did was amazing, and everything my younger brother did was sweet. Where did that leave me?

- **Youngest children** are often resented by their siblings for being pampered, babied and getting away with more than the others.

I come from a family of four boys. My youngest brother is six foot two and built like a tank, but my mother still does his washing and sends him food parcels. He's twenty-nine, for goodness' sake. Does it affect our relationship? Absolutely.

They can also be resented for copying their older siblings and getting the same privileges.

> *My younger sister felt she was entitled to do everything that I did. She insisted on going to bed at the same time as me and we had the same amount of pocket money. I didn't get any credit for being three years older and a lot more responsible.*

But youngest children often feel disgruntled because they're ordered around by their siblings, have to fetch and carry for everyone, or only get the last sliver of their busy parents' attention.

Circumstances Affect Their Relationship

Anything that upsets the balance of normal life or stresses you out can affect the way your children treat each other, from small things like packing to go on holiday, to major family upsets like divorce or moving house. There are countless circumstances that can change their relationship, but what you can't predict is what the effect is going to be. Hard times can make siblings closer, but they can also drive a wedge between them. If your children aren't getting on well, it's worth looking at what else might be going on.

They Almost Certainly Live Together

Unfortunately, one of the most obvious reasons for sibling conflict is the one you can't do anything about: they're under each other's feet all the time. In and out of the bathroom, round the breakfast table and – worst of all – crammed together into the back seat of the car.

Most siblings can't help getting under each other's skin and know exactly how to wind each other up. Their issues get magnified because they are so sensitive to each other's moods and spend so much time together in a confined space.

🔉 *One of my daughters has terrible allergies and the others give her a really hard time about it. They can't stand hearing her snorting and blowing her nose all day.* 🔉

🔉 *My brother and I shared a bedroom. I wanted to go to bed early, but he always wanted to read. Even if he turned the light off, he intentionally made noises just to provoke me. He'd smuggle in packets of crisps and crunch them because he knew it drove me up the wall.* 🔉

Changes to the Status Quo

When they're going through a bad patch

Your child might be unhappy or angry for reasons totally unconnected with his siblings, but take his feelings out on them. When someone's had a bad day, they're often foul to the people closest to them. So he's more likely to squabble with them if he felt persecuted by a teacher or fell out with a friend, and he might be grumpy if he's feeling ill, overtired, overworked or needs something to eat.

A rush of hormones can also cause all sorts of stroppiness and tantrums, and paediatricians say that this explains a lot of toddler behaviour. Many parents are also surprised when their children start having pre-teen mood swings long before there's any outward sign of puberty.

🔉 *My daughter used to be so sweet to her brother. But when she turned ten, her teenage hormones started coming in. Now she's a nightmare. Whatever he says, she contradicts him in a tone of voice which says, 'You idiot!'* 🔉

Some children who are going through a tricky time are perfectly well behaved at school but take out their frustrations on their siblings. In a way, you can take it as a compliment that they can express themselves at home. Underneath it all, they know they're loved and that you'll all still be there, whatever happens.

When there are changes to the routine
Even relatively minor changes to daily life can affect your children's relationships. One child may have a friend over to play and completely ignore his sibling. You may be working longer hours, so there's less of you to go round. Even a sibling's birthday can cause problems. Of course each child knows his own birthday will come too, but he doesn't like the way the other is suddenly getting most of the attention. Just because these are everyday issues doesn't mean they won't affect your children.

Stressful Events

Holidays
Issues get magnified further when siblings spend more time together than normal. Lots of parents complain that when school holidays begin, their children start fighting. Without the structure of the school day, there are acres of time to fill, so their children get bored and start bothering their siblings.

Some parents also dread going on holiday with their children. Quite apart from the packing, the thought of being cooped up with them in the car or on a plane can be overwhelming. What's the point of all the hassle and money spent on a holiday if they're just going to pick on each other?

Moving house
Moving house is such a pain. Apart from all the practical issues, it can shake up some strong feelings. If your children no longer feel rooted and safe, all sorts of complicated emotions are bound to surface.

My husband got a new job and we had to move further north. It really affected our children and they started fighting horribly. The new house was bigger and, after years of begging, for the first time they could each have their own bedroom. But I couldn't believe it. Despite all the arguing, they insisted they still wanted to share. **9**

New baby

A classic source of sibling rivalry is, of course, a new baby. The older child's position gets usurped and everyone's preoccupied with the little one.

When I was six, my brother was born, and my father was overjoyed that he was a boy. When he came home from work, he'd go straight to the baby. **9**

Sometimes the anger takes a bit of time to surface.

Josh wasn't that interested in his sister when she was tiny, so I didn't think we had a problem. But when she got older, he took against her.
The problem is he's quite rough. He smacks her if she touches his things. Yesterday he pushed her backwards and she gashed her head on the corner of the coffee table. **9**

Divorce and step-families

Divorce is stressful for everybody. The family gets ripped apart, and both adults and children can feel profoundly miserable and angry about it. Obviously this can have a huge impact on sibling relationships.

For the last six months, since we decided to get divorced, my son won't talk at mealtimes and always has his nose buried in a book. He used to play with his sister for hours in the garden. But now he shuts us all out. **9**

Not all parents remarry, but if they do, there can be fireworks when step- and half-families are thrown together.

My children used to get along OK, but life has been absolute hell since my husband's daughters moved in. My younger son clashes with them over absolutely everything. My older son can't stand it, so he has effectively moved out and spends all his time with his friends. It's just awful. He's only thirteen and he never wants to come home.

When One Child Needs More of Your Time

When one child has a time-consuming hobby

Sometimes one child takes up more of your time because he has a particular interest or talent, and it seems right to support him. You may spend hours driving to and from ballet classes, gym competitions, or whatever. But it can make your other children resentful.

I'm fed up with watching my sister in her county choir. She has so many rehearsals and performances and I'm sick of being dragged along too.

When one child has special needs

It can be difficult and time consuming for the whole family if one child has special needs, whether it's a learning and behavioural issue like autism, or a learning and physical disability like cerebral palsy. Whatever it is, this child will almost certainly need more care and attention, and this can stir up all sorts of feelings in the others. If they recognize how much their sibling needs you, they may not be outwardly resentful or angry, but their feelings deserve to be listened to.

My sister was severely disabled. My parents already had so much to deal with, I couldn't ever complain or make a fuss. I knew I had to be responsible and help them look after her. I resented it, because it was all about her and never about me.

Often the feeling is also one of disappointment, or longing for what might have been.

My brother has severe Down's syndrome, so there's a lot we can't do together. My best friend has a sister. They have matching bedrooms in the attic and they fight all the time, even though they have nothing to fight about. More than anything I wish I had a sister and matching bedrooms in the attic. If I did, I'd never fight with her at all.

One indicator of mild issues may be that a child doesn't interact with his siblings in the way you'd expect.

My son spends hours doing things by himself – he arranges his Warhammer figures and memorizes the flags of every country in the world.

He doesn't play games with his brothers or share any of their interests, and they find his obsessions really odd. They leave him out and though he doesn't seem to mind, I worry about him all the time.

I've asked his teacher about it and she thinks he might be mildly autistic. So we're going to have him properly assessed.

When Siblings Freeze Each Other Out

Lots of parents are worried about their children not because they fight, but because they hardly interact. You may wish your children played, got into mischief together or even occasionally took each other's side against you so you'd know they had some sort of meaningful relationship. If your children don't engage as much as you'd like, you may be disappointed. The causes are probably a combination of family circumstances and your children's individual characters. Here are some of the issues you might be facing.

One child may be the odd one out

If you have more than two children, there are probably times when at least one of them feels left out. It might be temporary, but if he's by far the oldest or the only one who doesn't like football in a family of sports fanatics, he may end up as the gooseberry.

My middle daughter is definitely the odd one out. The others get on so well that she ends up doing lots of stuff on her own. Seeing her by herself makes me so sad.

They may be screen addicts

You might worry that your children never communicate. But have you counted how many hours they're sitting in front of the computer and television? Studies show that British children are spending up to six hours a day staring at screens, so it's no wonder they aren't interacting with their siblings.

One child may have other interests

Children don't necessarily want to spend all their time with their siblings. Sometimes they want time on their own. If your child is into listening to music or has a lot of homework, he'll probably lock himself in his bedroom. Lots of teenagers will talk for hours with their friends, but when their family is around they just grunt and leave.

One child may prefer being an observer

Some children are happier on the sidelines, watching the action, daydreaming or doing their own thing. But if one of yours doesn't interact much, you may worry about him and keep trying to get him to join in. It's worth remembering that he may not be feeling left out at all.

One child may deal with issues by blocking everyone out

It's more of a worry if your child prefers to be alone because he's not happy. Some children shout or complain when they're upset, but there are plenty who withdraw into a world of their own. They want to be left alone because that's how they deal with their feelings.

My children usually get along pretty well. But Sam started coming home from school, going straight to his bedroom and closing the door. My daughter was miserable because he wasn't talking to her and she didn't know what she'd done. It turned out that it was nothing to do with her – he was being picked on by some boys on the bus.

Sometimes children feel excluded because a sibling has a closer relationship with their parents. Often they'll withdraw and ignore their sibling rather than fight for attention.

One child may use silence as a weapon

Some children don't interact because they know it annoys their siblings. They might refuse to talk simply to wind them up and get attention. But other children refuse to communicate because it's the only ammunition they have. As one child told us:

My brother is six years older than me and he's really horrible. He puts his feet on me when we're watching TV and repeats what I say in a stupid voice. He won't stop and I can't fight him. So I completely ignore him or walk away. There is nothing else I can do.

How Fighting Might Even Be Good for Your Children

There are all sorts of reasons your children might not be getting on, and we'll be showing you plenty of ways you can help them. But it's also worth remembering that sibling fights aren't always a complete disaster. There are plenty of reasons why friction between them might even be a good thing. Here's why:

They May Actually Enjoy It

When our children fight, we might find it incredibly stressful and blanch at some of the terrible things they say and do to each other. But they may be perfectly happy about it.

I had three sisters, and we used to bicker a lot. 'You did this . . . she took that . . . you said this . . . she said that.' My mother would come in looking really upset and make us stop. We'd be absolutely amazed. We were having a lovely time!

When children are wrestling (one in a headlock, another in a half nelson and the third whooping and jumping on them both), it might look as if they are killing each other. But for some children it's a way of showing affection and letting off steam. If they know how far to take it, scrapping and scuffling can be a normal part of childhood.

Lots of children would rather trade insults than sit in silence on a boring car journey. They like the attention they get from their siblings and seeing how close to the line they can get.

I can't believe some of the things my children say to each other: 'You old freakface', 'You're a complete jerk', 'Your bum stinks'. I'd hate it if anyone talked like that to me. But they seem to like it. The more they insult each other, the more they laugh.

As long as the teasing isn't upsetting either child, the bickering doesn't turn into bullying and no one's getting hurt, you can probably relax. In fact, if they're enjoying themselves you might not be able to keep them apart.

I often say to my children, 'There are six empty rooms in this house. Why are you both in this one fighting?'

They're Honest with Each Other

If your child's feet smell, his outfit looks terrible or if he has behaved like a complete idiot, his siblings will probably be the first to let him know. They might not be tactful about it, and he might hate them for it, but he may actually be relieved they've told him.

My teenage son wanted his hair cut really short. But when he got back from the barber it looked pretty bad. I told him it was fine, but his sister didn't mince her words. 'Urgh. You look like a nine-year-old skinhead.' Unfortunately, she was right.

She actually did him a big favour. He realized super-short hair really doesn't suit him, so he's growing it out.

They May Be Learning Life Skills

Growing up with siblings isn't always easy, but it's also an incredible learning experience. Home is the perfect place to begin to gauge what behaviour is acceptable and what isn't. It's safe and they're going to get honest, sincere feedback.

Sibling disagreements can teach children all sorts of things – how to stick up for themselves, negotiate, compromise and share. Your children might not always be able to work out their differences, but when they do, it can bring them closer together.

> My children were arguing in the car about iPod headphones. One was broken, so they both wanted the set that worked and insisted it belonged to them.
>
> This went on for fifteen minutes, round and round. Suddenly, the noise stopped. I couldn't believe it. In my rearview mirror I could see them, heads together, sharing the iPod with one earpiece each.
>
> Even more of a miracle, that weekend they pooled their money and bought a second set.

Arguing may not be as bad for your children as you might think.

> My parents never argued, and if I ever argued with my sister, they were so shocked it was as if the world had caved in. So we never did.
>
> Now I'm an adult I can't stand confrontation. My boss shouted at me one day at work and I started shaking and panicking.
>
> My best friend grew up in this big, noisy family, and this kind of thing doesn't bother her in the least. She says she knows she can stand up for herself.

Whatever the sibling dynamic in your family, there's almost certainly room for improvement. But what can you do? We'll start by showing you how to tackle classic issues like jealousy and resentment.

3

Dealing with Jealousy, Competitiveness and Resentment

By Improving Your Relationship with Your Children

Even sympathetic parents find it hard to understand how siblings can resent each other so much. After all, you're doing your best to love them all, and surely they should love each other too. But have you ever thought how it can feel to a child to have to share you?

Why Children Get So Jealous of Their Siblings

Here's a great insight into sibling rivalry, adapted from *Siblings Without Rivalry* by Adele Faber and Elaine Mazlish. It's from the perspective of a woman being married to a man, so apologies if your set-up is different. Imagine that:

Your husband says he loves you so much he's decided to get . . . another wife.
How would you feel? _____

His new wife is very attractive. When you go out together, people carry on about how adorable she is. When they ask what you think of her:
What's your first reaction? _____

You're upset and crying, and when your husband walks into the room you shout, *'I can't stand your new wife and I don't want her in this house any more. Why don't you just get rid of her!'*
When he says:

1. 'How can you be so horrible? She hasn't done anything to you.'
2. 'You're lucky – she'll always be here to keep you company.'
3. 'Stop complaining. You know I love you both the same.'
4. 'You know I can't get rid of her. We're a family now.'

How do you feel? _____

Interesting isn't it? You might feel a whole range of emotions, from defeated and abandoned to threatened and enraged. According to the authors, people often said they felt 'the burning desire to do harm, no matter what the cost. They wanted to get the newcomer into trouble, to hurt her physically . . . What's more, they wanted to hurt their mates too, to punish them for inflicting this misery upon them.' Suddenly a child's jealousy of a sibling or anger towards their parents doesn't seem so hard to understand.

But it's not always older children who feel threatened by a newcomer. Lots of younger children feel overshadowed by and venomous towards their siblings.

> *My toddler can't stand it if I pay attention to her older brother. Just yesterday he and I were sitting on the sofa talking. When she saw us, she climbed on to the sofa and squeezed in between us. Then she leaned up against me and told him to go away. He didn't, so she started pushing him on to the floor with her feet.*

Children can carry on being jealous when they're older. An incident that seems trivial to us (someone got a microscopically bigger cupcake or five minutes longer on the computer) can seem monumental to them. You may be able to solve this kind of problem by handing over another one or ensuring toys and computer time are distributed evenly. But the cause of the dispute can be something deeper: it can go back to your child's visceral resentment at having to share you. If the cupcake, computer time or whatever it is becomes a symbol of your love and attention, subconsciously that smaller portion can mean you love her less and all sorts of feelings can get stirred up.

If your children are competitive, they're absolutely normal and wired up perfectly: they've got the gene for basic survival. They need you to love them and look after them, and they'll do whatever it takes to ensure that you do. This evolutionary survival instinct runs deep, but, of course, you do love them. So what do you do if your children have everything they need but they're still jealous? The answer is to work on your relationship with each of them individually.

Improving Your Relationship with Your Children

Anything you can do to build a stronger, more meaningful relationship between you and your children will help. This might still seem illogical. After all, what does their arguing have to do with you? They're the ones who aren't getting along. You didn't tell them to kick each other under the table, snatch each other's toys or snarl, 'Get out of my room, you freak.' In fact, you've probably been begging them to be nicer to each other.

But if the cause of their animosity goes back to jealousy, you need to unlock and dissipate it. This will be much easier if they feel they can talk to you and are confident that you're on their side. Here's what you can do:

- **Make them feel more secure**
  When each child feels they're connected to you, it's like giving them the Ready Brek glow. If they feel good about themselves, they're less likely to be competitive.

- **Resolve their feelings**
  If each child knows you'll give them a fair hearing, they're more likely to confide in you. By listening, you can help them to

process their angry, resentful feelings before they take them out on each other.

- **Give them advice**
  If each can trust you don't love their sibling more, they're more likely to listen when you need to mediate between them.

Here are seven simple ways to make all this happen, so you can untangle jealousy, competitiveness and resentment.

Stand Back and Stay Calm
Try being a PAUSE PARENT

The place to start is by pausing. You'll have a better chance of building a good relationship with each child if you don't say things you regret when you're stressed. It's almost impossible if you shout at or criticize them a lot. No one can be perfectly reasonable and rational all the time, but **Pause Parents** are good at staying quiet, even when they're extremely aggravated. Of course they can get wound up like the rest of us when their children argue, but instead of blurting out unkind comments or spiralling out of control, they somehow stay calm. They know that taking a few deep breaths, counting to ten or walking out of the room can be so much more effective than shouting or saying something hurtful.

So how do **Pause Parents** do it?

Zip your lip If you're not a natural **Pause Parent**, one of the most important things you can do to improve your relationship with your children is to zip your lip and say nothing when you're feeling frazzled.

I was driving my children to school. We were late, the traffic was terrible and my son started singing a particularly tuneless rap song and jabbing his sister's leg with a pencil. She started singing another song even louder and punching him back. I asked them six times to stop.

When that didn't work, I shouted at them. Then when they still carried on, I roared, 'SHUT UP! You're so selfish! Just SHUT UP! I can't stand either of you!'

I was so shocked that I'd lost control like that, particularly over something so minor. I was so loud I actually gave myself a sore throat. And how could I have said that to my own children? That's not the sort of childhood I want them to have, being screamed at by a crazy woman. 🌀

We'd all like to think we can stay calm in the face of extreme provocation. Unfortunately, some children are experts at hooking us in and it can be near impossible to stay quiet and ignore them. Before you know it, you can find you get sucked in and react in a way that isn't helpful to you or your child.

🌀 *My daughter knows exactly how to make me angry. If I ask her to do anything, pick up her laundry or turn off the PlayStation, she wants to get into a debate about it. 'WHY-EE? Give me one good reason. Ha, you can't think of one, can you Mum?' It is really infuriating. First she gets a good ten minutes of me ranting, then I lose my temper and send her to her room. I hate it. It doesn't seem right that every conversation we have is an argument. Why can't we just talk about normal things?'* 🌀

Whether your children are arguing, or trying to drive you up the wall, it can be really helpful to try zipping your lip. So stay quiet, practise your deep breathing or walk into another room. This is particularly effective if one child tends to annoy you more than the others. If you don't react, she'll soon find it's no fun provoking you. Even better, because you aren't reacting in the same old way, which escalates the tension, your relationship with your child will start to change.

But if you lash out at her, she'll get resentful or take the things you say very personally. Often we don't mean to be harsh; we're irritable with our children simply because we're tired or over-stretched. But they don't know that.

If I did something by accident, like dropping a glass or spilling my food, my mother usually got angry with me. 'You're so clumsy,' she'd say, 'I can't trust you to do anything right.' She'd really upset me. I was quite a well-behaved child and never meant to do anything wrong. After a while I toughened up against her so her criticism wouldn't hurt me. I kept well away from her if I could.

If your child is sensitive, your tone of voice and emotions can be magnified, as though you're talking through a megaphone.

My daughter takes everything personally. When I tell all my children to hurry up or tidy something, tears often come to her eyes and she'll say, 'But why are you shouting at me?' I often need to take her to the side and reassure her that I'm not angry.

Whether your child is thin-skinned or not, you can't improve your relationship if she feels you're picking on her all the time. If you pause instead and give yourself time to think what you're going to say and how you're going to say it, you probably won't sound so critical.

Wait until later **Pause Parents** make life easy for themselves by waiting and tackling problems after everyone has calmed down. They don't react instantly or jump to conclusions about who is to blame, come down harder on one child or snap out unreasonable punishments. So they're far less likely to end up with a bunch of indignant children who feel they're being treated unfairly. Even if one child is being particularly foul towards either her parents or siblings, the same applies: they wait until later, when everyone can have a reasonable conversation.

Expect to get wound up **Pause Parents** know it's far easier to stay quiet if you can anticipate the things your children do that provoke you.

Bedtime is the worst. When we're all tired, I can't stand the noise or sheer pointlessness of their bickering. Why can't they just be nice to each other? And, of course, there's the fear underneath that one of them will really get hurt.

I have to keep reminding myself that they'll be fine, and I'll be fine, once they're all asleep.

There are all sorts of good reasons why we overreact. Children arguing and annoying each other sets most parents off, and some parts of the day are typically worse than others, like trying to get your children out of the door or into bed. But if you're ready for them, it's easier to stay in control and the whole situation is less of a big deal for everybody.

Keep things in perspective Instead of panicking that their children are going to damage each other for life, **Pause Parents** stay calm by keeping things in perspective. They realize that, in most cases, eventually the fighting really does end. Even if your children get along appallingly and you're convinced they hate each other, the relationship is repairable and we're going to give you all sorts of ideas about how you can help them. They may even surprise you and be fonder of each other than you realize.

From the time they were little, my oldest daughter, Laura, has been incredibly jealous of her little sister. I thought she hated her.

When Laura was chosen to sing a solo in a school concert, her music teacher told her to imagine she was singing it to her favourite person in the world. She surprised me and said she was singing it to her younger sister!

Now when they fight I don't always assume the worst.

Parents can easily get so fixated on small things that it can drive a wedge between them and their children. Sometimes we need to be reminded of what really matters.

My daughter drives me crazy. She leaves a mess everywhere she goes. She sheds clothes and shoes all over the house, and after her bath she leaves oozing shampoo bottles and wet towels everywhere. Sometimes I think I'm going to explode if I find her hair all over the bath again.

But my friend's son just had to have an operation. What's a messy bathroom compared to that?

Taking Things Personally

It's hard to keep things in perspective if you take them personally.

It sounds ridiculous. But when my baby won't eat the food I've so lovingly cooked and puréed, it really gets to me. I can't help it, but I feel she's rejecting me.

My son said that I was completely useless. The worst mother in the world. It made me cry.

My mother is still going on about all the horrible things I said to her when I was a teenager. I can't remember what I said, but she took everything I said to heart. It's unbelievable, but she's still angry and upset about it.

Parents can also take it personally when their children don't get along as well as they'd like.

When my children fight it depresses me and I beat myself up for being a terrible mother. The more they fight, the more I feel like a failure.

If your children don't behave the way you want or if they say unkind things, it's very natural to take it to heart. So if you're feeling sensitive or the comments are getting to you, try to zip your lip until you can calm down. Then either you'll realize it wasn't such a big deal, or that you can discuss it later.

Listen to Feelings
Try being a TUNED-IN PARENT

Tuning in is one of the most powerful ways to help your children feel closer to you, and they'll get on better with each other if they don't feel they need to fight for your approval. If you're tackling intense sibling feelings, like resentment, you probably can't do without it.

- **Tuned-In Parents** try to understand the feelings behind their children's behaviour. They know unresolved feelings are often the cause of sibling rivalry, so if their children treat each other appallingly, they try to find out what's going on underneath.

- **Tuning-In** also puts you in a better position to help defuse sibling arguments. If your children feel you listen to them, in return they're more likely to listen to you when you have to be the referee. Further, the more you understand what lies at the root of their problems, the easier it is to help them.

Listen and accept difficult feelings Listening to your children can work wonders, but it isn't always easy. When they have strong feelings about their siblings, they can sound bratty, unreasonable and irritating. You know the kind of comments we mean:

- *'No, that's mine!'*
- *'He's annoying me on purpose.'*
- *'I HATE her.'*

Often our first instinct is to make them stop complaining as quickly as possible by telling them to be quiet:

- *'Oh for heaven's sake, STOP MOANING!'*
- *'Shush! I don't ever want to hear you talking like that.'*

Or we try to cheer them up by telling them it doesn't really matter:

- *'Come on, sweetheart. It's not so bad.'*
- *'Never mind, I'm sure she didn't mean it.'*

Sometimes this is enough to stop them from fussing, but long term it isn't a good idea. When you don't listen properly or you're dismissive, they can get frustrated and may even begin to resent you.

When I was five I walked into the living room and my sister bashed me on the head with her recorder. I started crying and told my father. He said I shouldn't have gone in there because she was practising.

I said, 'But I didn't know what she was doing.' He told me to be quiet and stop making such a big deal of it.

Years later and I'm still annoyed at my sister for hitting me on the head. But I'm even more annoyed with my dad for not listening to my side of the story or caring how I felt.

Children find it very comforting when you listen, because they feel understood. It helps to acknowledge how they're feeling by putting it into words.

So instead of:

- *'For goodness' sake, it's not the end of the world. She didn't mean to spill her drink on you,'*

try:

- *'Yes, your dress is all wet and I know how badly you wanted to wear it.'*

Sometimes you can't resolve their complaints easily. If it's not appropriate to put your children to bed at the same time, for example, at least listen and show you understand how your child feels about it.

So instead of:

- *'Oh for the last time! She goes to bed later than you because she's much older than you. And she'll always be older than you, so just get used to it,'*

try:

- 'I know how much you hate having to go to bed earlier. It's hard being the youngest.'

Going towards your child's unhappiness and accepting it, instead of pushing it away, can seem strange if you've never done it before. You may worry that it will actually make things worse and she'll become even more upset and unreasonable. But you might be staggered how effective it can be.

> My son was always such a cry-baby. He'd whine constantly. His older sisters couldn't stand spending time with him and, to be frank, neither could I. I hated to see him upset, but his whingeing was really embarrassing, so I was always telling him to stop it. But it wasn't working. In fact, if anything, he was getting worse.
>
> One weekend we went to lunch at some friends' and he complained about everything: the other children were bouncing too hard on the trampoline, he didn't like the cats and he didn't want potatoes. Then he started crying because a fly landed near his plate. I was so embarrassed and my daughters announced – out loud – that he had cried thirty-two times while we were there.
>
> I asked the other mother what I should do, and she suggested being sympathetic and acknowledging how he felt. She said she'd learned to do it at a parenting class and it was a bit of a miracle-worker. 'Say, "Oh I see, you didn't like that fly coming near you." Then he'll know you understand him and he'll stop trying so hard to get you to listen to him.' It sounded a bit mad, but nothing else was working so I decided to try it.
>
> The amazing thing was, she was right. He's so much happier. I feel terrible for not listening to the poor little guy sooner.'

'But my children say such terrible things about each other.'

When a child says she hates her sibling it can be hard to stomach. If you wouldn't like the idea of sharing your spouse, perhaps you can understand how she feels, but it can still go against all your instincts to allow her to express it. So even if you see the point of tuning in to feelings, in practice you might be doing something very different.

- You might be tempted to teach your child what's acceptable:

  'Darling – don't speak like that about your sister.'

- You might try to tell her she's mistaken:

  'You don't hate her. She's your little sister and you'll love her for ever.'

- You might try to calm her down:

  'It's not so bad. I'm sure she didn't mean it.'

- You might just be angry:

  'How dare you speak like that about her! Go to your room.'

If you try to squash your child's feelings it can be very frustrating for her. It's fine telling her she can't hit or hurt her siblings, but if she isn't even allowed to dislike them, you can end up with a problem. Trying to make sense of complicated emotions is difficult enough for a child. If you also keep telling her that she should love her siblings, she can feel guilty, ashamed or angry on top.

When you're trying to encourage family unity, allowing a litany of abuse about one of your children can make it seem as if you're going about it backwards. But at the time, your angry child might think she absolutely does hate her sibling. If you suppress or deny her feelings, she may convince herself she'll hate him FOR EVER, just to spite you. She may also be angry with you for not under-standing her. Left festering and unprocessed, complicated layers of resentment can build up.

But if you listen, she'll let them go more quickly. So even if her feelings are explosive, it's best to let her express them. Do whatever it takes to stay quiet, even if you find her emotions overwhelming. It helps to remember that you're just helping her vent her feelings so she doesn't take them out on her siblings.

Ironically, the more you accept your children's angry feelings towards each other, the more likely they are to get along. Once they're out in the open, they'll begin to dissipate and no longer overshadow their whole relationship. Here are four other very good reasons for tuning in.

To ensure each child feels loved and understood

Tuning in can prevent so many problems from escalating. When your child feels misunderstood, she's more likely to defy you. This is one reason why tiny little issues between the two of you can somehow turn into raging arguments. If she also thinks you get on better with her sibling, she can assume her sibling is the favourite and you don't love her as much. If she's resentful about it, she might start distancing herself from you, or she might take out her frustration on her sibling by niggling at him, hitting him or trying her hardest to get him punished.

❦ *I felt my mother always indulged my younger sister but criticized me. When she was a toddler, I got jealous and was desperate to get her into trouble. I remember opening my mother's make-up drawer and squirting swirls of red make-up all over her dressing table, as though my sister had done it. Then I told my mother I'd seen her mess everything up. My plan worked.* ❦

But if you listen to both siblings, they'll both feel less inclined to be competitive.

To help your angry child

You may have a child you feel is out of control, and you may be right. Perhaps she has temper tantrums or lashes out at her siblings. But maybe she's angry because she feels completely misunderstood. She may be unable to express herself properly or get you to hear what she is trying to tell you. Her frustration, sadness or regret that she doesn't have the relationship with you that she'd like can come out as anger.

> When I was little my parents used to tell everyone I was a trouble-maker. In some ways they were right. I scratched down the side of the car with a key and bashed a hole in our wooden fence with an axe. But I was just really, really angry.
>
> My parents had a great relationship with my older brother, but we didn't get along as well. I couldn't put it into words at the time, but my mother's best friend later told me she always suspected I'd felt really left out.

To put an end to bullying and mean behaviour

If you don't spend time tuning in to your children, you may never know what's really going on with them.

Siblings can get up to all sorts of awful things, so children need to know they can confide in their parents. It's up to us to know them well enough to detect when they are telling the truth or making up stories, or at least to have an inkling of what they're actually capable of doing to each other.

> When I was younger, my two older brothers tied me to a chair, left me there for hours and only untied me before our mother came home from work. When she got back I tried to tell her the whole story, but my brothers kept laughing and said I was making it up.
>
> It wasn't until I was in college that they finally owned up and told her what really happened.

Sometimes you can get the information you need only if you happen to ask the right question.

> I asked my three-year-old, 'So, how are you getting on with your big sisters?'
>
> He scowled. 'I don't like them. They're mean to me.'
>
> 'Oh,' I said, 'what don't you like?'
>
> 'I hate it when they bite the back of my legs,' he said.
>
> 'Why do they do that?' I asked, trying not to panic.
>
> 'Because then you won't notice when I'm in the bath.'
>
> I took a look at the back of his thighs and, sure enough, he had bite marks down them. I was horrified!

If you're always busy or seem very anxious, your children may not want to trouble you with their own worries.

My twin sister and I were the youngest of six. Our oldest brother told us we were going to be given up for adoption because our parents didn't have enough money. We worried about it secretly for years because we knew our parents were struggling to make ends meet.

Whether your children are upsetting each other with mild jokes and teasing, or physically bullying each other, you can't guarantee that they'll be able to handle it on their own. You need to know what's going on, and it's worth being alert to the possibility that one child needs your help but isn't asking for it. If she's being bullied, she may feel discouraged and defeated and think there's no point in complaining about it. She might be afraid the bullying will get worse if she gets her sibling into trouble, or assume that you don't want to know about it.

Our oldest brother used to terrorize us. My mother had no idea how to handle it and my father had a very important job. When he came home from work we were meant to be quiet and look after him, and not burden him with our own problems. So nothing was ever done about it.

Our parents died years ago and we're all in our fifties. But we still don't have a relationship with our oldest brother. Don't want to – and never will.

To help your child with other problems

The cause of your child's problems may be nothing to do with you or her siblings. If she's in trouble at school, finding it hard to make friends or being bullied, you'll probably feel the repercussions at home.

If you don't tune in and find out what's really going on, you might assume she's being rude and grumpy just to make everyone's life more difficult. By listening you may not be able to help her directly, but she should start to feel better and maybe begin to see her way through her troubles on her own. With your support, her problems won't seem so overwhelming and she'll almost certainly be nicer to have around. Even if her behaviour doesn't improve, you'll find it easier to be sympathetic and you can explain to the other children why they need to be kind to her.

'This tuning in sounds as if it's going to take a lot of time. But I don't have any time.'

Sometimes it seems impossible to give each child your full attention; life expands to fill every second we have, without a moment to spare.

> My parents had five children in five years. I felt they never had time to listen to me. It wasn't parenting. It was crowd control.

Working parents and divorced parents get a particularly tough deal.

> When I get home from work I've got shopping to unload, washing to fold, homework to supervise and phone calls to make. I don't have time for heart-to-hearts, there's too much I've got to do.

The good news is that you don't have to set aside acres of time, or take each child on special outings, to tune in. Of course you can block out the afternoon or spend money if you want to, but you can also listen to them simply by changing your mindset. Even if you're doing the dishes, you can give them your attention for a moment when they talk to you. Listening to your children's feelings can be far more efficient than letting them build up and then dealing with the fall-out. So you'll almost certainly save time in the long run.

You can listen to your children anywhere – in the car or even at the supermarket. It's possible to know your children well, even if the time you have together is limited.

My parents were divorced and we lived with our mum. I never felt that close to her. She was always busy doing everything for us, but she never really took the time to sit and chat or find out how we were feeling.

We only saw our father every other weekend, but when we did he was always interested in us. We felt we could tell him anything.

Once the floodgates are opened and your child gets used to letting you know what's going on, she's more likely to confide in you when she has a problem. True, it's usually when you're trying to do something else. But that's probably because you're always trying to do something else.

Lying

There'll be times when your children will need your help, so it's really important that they get into the habit of telling the truth. You can't help them if you don't know the full story.

Try being a Tuned-In Parent
The more you tune in and accept feelings, the less your children will feel the need to lie. They're more likely to be honest if they know you won't freak out or be judgemental when they mess up.

Our greenhouse window was broken. I had no idea how it happened and our children all denied it. Two days later our son confessed he'd done it with his cricket ball, but had been too scared to tell us. We were so proud of him for telling the truth we weren't angry with him for lying, and then he offered to pay for the glass.

I want all my children to know that if they come to us with a problem we'll listen and discuss it.

Tuning in when you find it hard to listen

Like anything new, tuning in may seem odd at first and may take some getting used to. This is especially true if your child has done something hideous and you just want to make sure it never happens again.

I couldn't believe it, I actually heard my seven-year-old tell her dad to f*** off! My husband went ballistic and tried to make her apologize, but she flatly refused, so eventually he sent her to bed.

The next day he told her that he wouldn't have language like that in the house and tried to make her apologize again, but she looked defiant and wouldn't talk to him.

I decided to try something different. When he had gone out, I said, 'I heard what you said to your dad. That's not like you. You must have been pretty upset about something.'

She said he'd been bugging her all day by grumbling and bossing her around. I kept listening and finally she said she thought she'd better say sorry.

Of course sometimes it's fine to confront your child directly, but you'll probably find it's easier if you tune in first. Deep down, children usually already know what they've done wrong, so they don't need, or want, us to point it out. If we tell them off before hearing their side, they'll probably get defiant and irritable and refuse to accept their part in it. But if we listen and give them the chance to offload their feelings, they can usually see for themselves where they've made their mistakes.

There are some parents who find tuning in difficult because of the way they were brought up themselves. They don't feel comfortable discussing or expressing strong feelings because it's never been part of their family culture. When you're new to tuning in, you might also be shocked by what your child says. If her feelings have been pent up for a long time, she may seem like a volcano erupting when her frustration and anger start coming out. You might hear some unpalatable truths, but if you keep letting her vent her emotions, she should calm down. Over time her outbursts won't be so violent, and as you get used to listening, you'll probably find her strong feelings less unnerving.

'Could tuning in be bad for my children?'

Some parents worry that if they tune in too much, their children will end up ultra-sensitive or wimpy.

> Our son kept crying at school and complaining at home, and his teacher suggested listening to him and giving him lots of sympathy and support. I thought it was a good idea. But my husband thought it was completely stupid. He said our son just needed to buck up and get on with it.

We all want our children to be resilient so they can handle whatever life throws at them. But if your child is upset, telling her to pull herself together is unkind. The best way to help her cope with her feelings is to tune in and take what she says seriously, and eventually she'll be able to manage them on her own.

Talking about your child's behaviour

If your child keeps whingeing or being rude or aggressive, it's hard not to talk about it, especially if you're worried about her. But it can really upset her if she overhears you going on about her faults to other people. So even if she's done something monstrous to her sibling, **Tuned-In Parents** don't rehash the incident in public to their friends, and particularly not to their other children.

> My mother is still telling everyone about the time I pushed my brother over and he dislocated his shoulder, and that was three years ago. She makes me SO angry.

Some parents intentionally talk out loud about their children to make excuses for them or to try to get them to change.

- *'These two would kill each other if I let them. How do you get yours to behave so beautifully?'*

- *'Don't pay any attention to Jack. He has these outbursts regularly.'*

But **Tuned-In Parents** know how humiliating it is for a child to feel criticized unfairly or gossiped about. Of course there are times when we all need advice or a chance to offload our feelings. But if you've got to talk to someone, choose a discreet friend and make sure there's no chance your child can overhear you.

'But my daughter is being so horrible to her brother I've got to talk to him about it. I can't just leave him to suffer.'

We aren't saying you should never talk to the other child who was involved. If the 'victim' wants to tell you what happened, of course you should listen to his side of the story. But don't disparage his sister, even if her behaviour was appalling. You can listen and concentrate on one child's feelings without passing judgements about the other.

So if he says:

- *'I hate my sister. I really hate her. She kicked a ball into my room on purpose and knocked over all the stuff on my desk. When I yelled at her, she called me a pustule,'*

try tuning in to show that you understand:

- *'I can see why you're angry. It's really annoying when your room gets messed up.'*

You might be astonished to find that this is enough to calm him down. The perpetrator almost certainly had her reasons too, so you should talk to her separately. If you don't accuse her and keep the conversation straightforward, she'll be more willing to make amends.

'My child doesn't need more love and understanding. He needs more boundaries. I don't want him to turn into a spoilt brat.'

Of course your child needs to know what behaviour is acceptable and what isn't, and there will be times when you need to be tough. But if you start by being understanding, she's more likely to listen to what you have to say and be more cooperative. It's worth remembering you're not spoiling her or letting her get away with anything, just trying to solve the problem.

Apologizing to Your Children

Reconnect We're all human and we all say and do things we regret. **Tuned-In Parents** know that the way to reconnect with our children when we make a mistake is to apologize. It's not grovelling; it's teaching them the right thing to do. It's also one of the best ways to let go of guilt and feel human again.

> *My children got into a big fight yesterday morning, and I handled it really badly. I said sorry later, but one of my daughters wasn't having any of it. She said I'd apologized the last time, which was true.*
>
> *All I could say was that I really do try. I wish I didn't make mistakes, but I do. After that she was fine about it.*

If the distance between you has been developing for quite some time, reconnecting might not be so easy, but your best way forward is to try being a **Tuned-In Parent**. Once your child feels you're making the effort to understand her, there's every chance she'll be more receptive.

Treating Your Children Differently

On the whole we don't mean to treat any of them differently, and half the time we don't even realize we're doing it. But it's worth considering what's going on in your family. Here are some very common situations.

When one child needs you more

Some parents feel very protective over one child and may worry more about her than about her siblings. She may be younger, quieter, weaker, less academic, less attractive, shorter, less popular, have a worse relationship with her other parent, or perhaps she was very ill as a baby and you can't bear to see her suffer now. She might bring out your nurturing instincts because she makes you feel more wanted. Or you might feel your other children have an advantage over her, so you need to boost her up.

I feel so sorry for my second son. When he competes against his brother, he's never going to win. He's so much younger and weaker. He's also not as clever at school. So I try to make things even by buoying him up and making a big fuss over him. If he gets twelve out of twenty on a spelling test, for example, I make a big deal about it to boost his confidence. But I won't say anything to my older son who gets much higher marks because I don't want to praise him in front of his younger brother.

When they fight I usually intervene. The little one can't stand up for himself and I have to be tough on the older one if he starts getting rough.

Being kind to your needy child is wonderful, but you won't be doing her any favours if it's at the expense of her siblings. By giving her special attention and protection, you can set up an unpleasant dynamic. The problem can quickly become circular; the child you set out to protect really will need a bodyguard if her siblings start getting jealous. Here's how you can inadvertently get into a vicious circle:

- *You protect your needier child more than the others.*
- *Her siblings start getting resentful, so they begin distancing themselves or being mean to her.*
- *Your heart bleeds for your ostracized, disadvantaged child. So you try to level the playing field by boosting her up and fighting her battles (some parents simultaneously try to hold their more advantaged children back).*
- *This winds up her siblings further. They become even more jealous and resentful and treat her even worse.*

❛ *My sister and I fought constantly. She was everyone's little pet favourite, and it drove me mad. So I always tried to beat her up.* ❜

Another unfortunate side effect is that your lack of confidence in her can affect her self-esteem. When you set out to help the underdog, you can send her the message that she isn't up to looking after herself. If she internalizes it, she may feel she can't manage without you or stand her ground. This kind of learned helplessness is not only bad for the child, but it can also alienate her siblings.

❛ *My brother has always relied on our parents for everything. When I finished school, I was expected to get a job and look after myself, which I've always done.*

But he runs home every time he has a problem. He recently got into an accident and needed a new car and, of course, my parents got him one. I don't know why I'm surprised. ❜

Some needy children do what they can to get out of the cycle and be self-sufficient, but it's not always easy.

My parents were overprotective and always did everything for me. Even though I'm nearly forty, things other people take for granted, like hanging a picture or cooking a meal for friends, still seem overwhelming.

The way my parents babied me drove my brother crazy, and he always blamed me. I don't think he'll ever realize how hard I've tried to be independent. He still makes snide comments and keeps his distance.

'But one of my children really does need me more than the others.'

There will almost certainly be times when one child needs you more, and you can't change the circumstances. If you have a new baby, for example, you can't ignore her just so her older sibling doesn't get jealous, but you can be sympathetic.

The baby's four months old, and her brother's gone back into nappies and is having temper tantrums. My heart goes out to him. He's had three years of being my baby, and it's hard for him to adjust.

Children who outwardly appear to be confident and self-reliant also need you, even if they don't show it.

My son has severe food allergies so I have to do a lot for him. Every morning I make him a lunch, and I always have to accompany him on school trips and to birthday parties in case he has an allergic reaction.

It doesn't bother my daughter at all. She's very independent and does almost everything for herself.

Your child might seem absolutely fine, but at a deeper level she might resent you giving so much extra time and attention to her sibling.

When you can't change your needier child's circumstances – perhaps because he's disabled or has other problems – and you suspect that your other child feels she's not getting enough of your time and attention, the key is to tune in to both of them. Instead of trying to help your needy child see the bright side of things, try accepting his frustration. It's far kinder and will help him cope better in the long run. Instead of ignoring your other child's jealousy, try accepting that she feels left out. This will help her process her feelings so that she doesn't turn into a seething pot of resentment. With luck, both children will feel more loved and understood.

When it's easier to be nicer to one child

It isn't unusual for parents to find they get along better with some of their children than others. If one is more affectionate, appreciative or has a good sense of humour, you may find her easier.

Lots of parents relate to the child who shares the same birth order in the family as they do. If you were the youngest and felt pushed around by your siblings, you might try to protect your youngest so she won't suffer like you did. If you were the middle child and felt your parents always sided against you, you might side with your middle child to redress the balance. Or maybe you were the oldest and felt you were given too much responsibility, so you try not to load too much on your first child.

Sometimes the relationship with one child can be more complicated. Perhaps you feel guilty because you didn't bond properly when she was a baby, or she was ill as an infant or you weren't able to spend as much time with her when she was little. If you have a niggling feeling that your other children got a better start in life or you didn't do your best for this one, you might find you're still trying to make it up to her.

Or you might find your own experiences when you were growing up influence the way you treat her.

❝ My mother and I had a terrible relationship and I refused to speak to her for three years when I was a teenager.

One of my daughters is very similar to me and when we argue, I panic. I'm extra nice to her and let her walk all over me because I worry she's never going to love me. I have to remind myself that every argument we have isn't a relationship-breaker. It helps to remember that my mother and I get on better now. ❞

Lots of parents find one child has them 'wrapped around her finger', and it's almost impossible to be tough or to say no to her. They may not even notice how much they favour her.

My husband totally spoils our daughter. She's super-sweet and in his eyes she's perfect. Every night when he gets home from work and sees her, his face lights up and he hugs her, chases her all around and bounces her up in the air. He is absolutely besotted. But he hardly pays any attention to our son, who's three years older. All he gets is a 'How ya doin', mate?'

If you fuss more over one child, *you* may not realize you're doing it, but her siblings definitely will. They can even get the message they're less lovable, not so special or don't deserve to be appreciated.

Being the child who is left out can be so painful. She can feel she's on the outside of the main parent–child relationship. Whether or not she shows it on the surface, all sorts of resentments can start building up. If she feels alienated or that the regime is unfair, she might simply refuse to have anything to do with either you or her sibling.

My mother always got on better with my sister than with me. Every time she was upset, my mother was there to comfort her and agree that I was a bully, even though my sister was stronger and taller than I was.

This has gone on for decades and now I try not to see either of them. I'm sick and tired of it being two against one.

When one child is talented
In some families all the attention goes to the gifted child. If you have a football star, a child on the chess circuit or a competitive gymnast, the amount of energy focused on that child, not to mention the to-ing and fro-ing, is endless.

My daughter has been asked to train for the national swimming team. We go to competitions all over the country and because they're at weekends, the whole family often has to go. We've all got to do what we can to support her.

The others may be proud of their sibling, but if they're perpetually dragged along or left behind so you can support her, they may begin to feel hard done by. Even if you've worked it out beautifully so they spend that time with friends or their grandparents, resentment can quietly start to worm its way into your family's relationships.

When you come down harder on one child

Instead of boosting one child up, it isn't unusual for parents to come down harder on one of their children. The most obvious reason is because she's difficult. It's hard to be kind and supportive to a child who is constantly rude and combative, especially if she's also horrible to her siblings. She may also tap into your visceral fears or unresolved feelings. Maybe you can't stand her anger. If it makes you feel out of control or unstable, you'll do anything you can to stop her. Or it could be that one child simply annoys you far more than her siblings do.

> *I know it isn't fair, but when my son defies me he makes me so angry. When his little sister does the same thing, I often think it's funny.*

Sometimes it's the child who's most like you that drives you mad. She may have similar habits, or character traits that you were criticized for or that you don't like in yourself.

> *I was a very dreamy, disorganized child. My son is the same and I'm on his back all the time trying to get him motivated. I can't help nagging him.*

You may feel one child has more going for her than her siblings and try to redress the balance.

> *My oldest daughter is really bright and won a scholarship to a private school. So I give her extra chores around the house. I don't want her to get big-headed or think she's any better than her brothers and sisters.*

Guilty feelings can also get in the way. You can feel guilty for just about anything, and get that sinking feeling every time you remember the trouble you had bonding with one child, breast-feeding or going back to work too quickly. As we've mentioned, some parents spoil the child associated with these feelings, but others find they become more distant.

If you're tougher on one child, don't think she won't notice. Even if you explain that you're doing it because she's older or has more going for her, she won't feel any better about it. Explanations won't work if she feels she's treated as a second-class citizen or that you love her less. If your other children also pick up on it, they might feel entitled to treat her badly as well, knowing you won't take her side.

In my family I honestly felt like Cinderella. I was the oldest girl so I had lots of chores and the others didn't have to lift a finger.

My brother also used to beat me up all the time and never got into trouble.

If these patterns echo anything that's going on in your family, don't be too hard on yourself. Just being aware that they exist will help. The more you understand how you feel about each one of your children, the easier it will be to change your relationship.

When children don't cooperate

Some parents find they have one particular child who'd rather answer back than do what she's told. Even though you love her as much as her siblings, if she consistently makes your life more difficult, it can be hard not to get irritated with her.

If my little one makes a mess in the kitchen, he'll clear it up. If I have to remind him, I get a 'Yes Mum', right away.

But my oldest leaves plates and apple cores in his room, crumbs and cheese all over the kitchen floor and kicks his trainers off wherever he feels like it. When I ask him to tidy up, he growls and complains, puts it off, or yells, 'Why should I? I'm sick of you nagging me the whole time.'

I get annoyed with him and he gets annoyed with me. It's definitely a strain on our relationship.

He also sees that I don't argue with his brother, and I suspect he resents us both for it. But what can I do? I can't be nastier to the little one just to make it fair.

Other parents find that it's not always the same child who is being difficult. Most children go through phases of being more or less annoying or defiant. But if their behaviour gets to you, it can be hard not to let it affect how you feel about them.

When I was a rebellious teenager, my parents used to go on and on at me. I couldn't understand why they made such a big deal about everything.

Now I've got children of my own, I can see why it happened. Life is difficult and complicated enough on normal days. When one child is digging in his heels and making my life more complicated, it's hard to be nice to him.

If one child doesn't do what you ask, you can easily end up being unfair to her because she annoys you.

One of my children is going through a very trying phase. I'm sure she enjoys winding me up on purpose by refusing to do what she's told. When the others come running to me complaining about her, I should give her a fair hearing. But often I assume that she's the cause of those arguments too, and side against her.

What you can do if you treat your children differently

Try being a TUNED-IN PARENT

As your children are all different, it's almost inevitable that you'll feel differently about them. It's also not surprising that sometimes one child requires more of your attention. But if one of your children feels she's treated worse than her siblings, it's another classic trigger for resentment and jealousy. So what can you do? Again, start by tuning in as much as you can. By listening, you can untangle her feelings and ensure that each of your children feels connected to you. If tuning in isn't working as well as you'd like, we'll give you some more ideas below.

Getting your child to open up

With some children it's quite easy to tune in to their feelings because they'll come and tell you exactly what's going on and how they feel about it. But with others it can be much harder. They might find it difficult to discuss their feelings and insecurities; the more you pry, the more they clam up.

The sibling who needs you the most is often the difficult child who puts on the most convincing act that she doesn't. Unfortunately, this is also the child who is usually the hardest to get through to. Either she refuses to talk to you, or when she tells you how she feels she's so horrible about it that she pushes you away. If you're feeling 'allergic' to one child, as if you can't wait to get away from her, it's actually a big clue that she really needs your help. As the actress Nanette Newman told her daughters: 'The times you like your children the least are the times they need you to love them the most.'

Some children seem very independent, or even unfeeling and callous, as if they don't need you at all. Though all evidence may point to the contrary, this type of child has feelings too. Their self-sufficient front might be a defence mechanism, covering up what's really going on inside. They're busy convincing themselves and you that they don't need you and don't care, but a child like this might actually need you to take the time to listen and understand her even more than your others do.

Some children get discouraged because you haven't listened in the past or because you've made such a big deal about their problems that they don't want to upset you. So they may not think it's worth telling you how they feel. Whatever the reason, it's really annoying when you're ready to tune in to your child but she refuses to tell you what's going on. You might even feel that she's refusing to talk on purpose simply to irritate you. But this usually isn't the whole story.

❝ *My daughter was really upset with me last night, but she blanked me and wouldn't discuss it. This morning she wouldn't talk to me at all on the way to school.*

I finally forced her to tell me what was wrong by threatening she could walk with the neighbours in future if she was going to ignore me. I didn't feel very good about my tactics, but how else was I supposed to find out why she was upset?

Turns out she was jealous because I'd been concentrating on getting her brother ready for scout camp. We've been talking about it for weeks and yesterday I bought him all sorts of new equipment for the trip. ❞

What can you do to open the lines of communication? Long term, try making a point of chatting to your children about all sorts of things – what's happened at school, what they'd like to do at the weekend, what they think of the television programme you're watching, or whatever else they'd like to talk about. By being interested in their opinions and what's going on in their lives, you can begin to build a relationship that's special to each one of them. The more you listen without passing judgement, the more likely they are to come to you when they have a problem with school, their siblings or anything else.

❝ *My daughter used to insist she didn't like talking about her feelings, and it was frustrating. But I started focusing on her and listening whenever she did talk. Before I knew it she was talking all the time, telling me everything. She doesn't even realize she's doing it.* ❞

Encouraging Your Child to Talk

Try being a Pause Parent

Even if you're desperate to get information out of your child, try not to pressure her into talking. If she thinks you're being nosy, she'll clam up. Instead, wait until later. Lots of children don't want to rehash their day the moment they get home from school but are happy to tell you later on.

Try being a Tuned-In Parent

To encourage her to talk, neutral statements work better than direct questions. Try:

- *'It looks like something happened today at school.'*

Try being a Cheerleader Parent

She's more likely to chat if she doesn't feel criticized, so notice and comment on anything your child does right.

Try being a Commando Parent

Let her know that she can come to you if she wants to. Try:

- *'I know something has been bothering you and you haven't wanted to talk about it. But I'm here to listen if you need me.'*

Try being a Physical Parent

Give her a hug, or a back, head or foot massage. If she feels closer to you, she's more likely to confide how she feels.

Try being a Laid-Back Parent

Ask for her thoughts on all sorts of things, from choosing bedtime stories to suggestions about the family holiday, so she gets the feeling you're interested in her opinions and trust her judgement. Then she'll find it easier to talk about the things that matter to her.

'My child usurps all my attention and demands so much of my time the others hardly get a word in.'

For some children, tuning in seems to be the last thing they need. They want more and more attention from you and will push their siblings out of the way to get it.

This type of child can be incredibly annoying. She's constantly in your face, tugging on your arms and forcing you to acknowledge her. She may get her way more than her siblings because she's very expressive and makes such a big noise about everything.

> *When I walk my children to school, my daughter won't let go of me. She won't let my other children hold my hand or get a word in edgeways. She always demands my attention and it drives me mad.*

This child may seem like an empty hole that can't be filled. Although you may feel you're doing everything you can to listen to her, you might feel so irritated that you're subconsciously doing the opposite and pushing her away. Unfortunately she can probably pick up on your ambivalence, which may make her even more clingy.

So instead of trying to get her to separate from you, the way to solve this problem is actually to go towards it. Instead of trying to prise yourself away from her grasp, try taking her seriously and listening. It's rather like a Mexican finger trap, the type you might find in a toyshop. It's a little woven tube, and you stick your index fingers into it from opposite ends. Then you try to pull them out. But the harder you pull, the tighter it gets. The trick is to relax your fingers and move them gently towards each other. Then it loosens up straight away.

Try consciously tuning in so that you understand what's actually going on inside her. Is she insecure? Does she genuinely need more nurturing from you before she can move on developmentally? Once your child feels she's got what she needs, she'll be less annoying to both you and her siblings.

'Are you sure all this tuning in is a good idea? My mother used to drive me mad by prying into my feelings all the time.'

Taking the time to listen to your children can help enormously. But some people say they've been put off deep conversations for life because their parents wouldn't stop asking questions and picking issues apart. If your children really don't want to talk about their feelings, it's best not to force it. There are plenty of other things you can do to strengthen your relationship. You could start by being a **Cheerleader** and giving your children lots of praise.

Notice the Good, Ignore the Rest
Try being a CHEERLEADER PARENT

Cheerleader Parents are very positive. They focus on the wonderful things their children do and try to ignore the rest. Being a **Cheerleader Parent** is a fantastically effective way to strengthen your relationship with each one of your children. By encouraging them, you can help them feel appreciated and reassure them you're on their side.

If you try being a **Cheerleader Parent**, your children are more likely to get on better too. When you give them each plenty of attention, you can help diminish competitive feelings between them.

- By praising them, they'll feel better about themselves and won't feel the need to squash each other down or vie so hard for your attention.
- By showing you've noticed when they're nice to each other, they'll begin to see themselves as siblings who get along.

Cheerleader Parents are also amazing at giving their children compliments without making them feel competitive. This is an incredible skill, and we'll show you how they do it.

Praising your children instead of nagging

Notice the good, ignore the bad However good our intentions, it's not always easy to focus on what children are doing right, especially when they bicker, moan and fight. Their arguing can take up your whole field of vision; you may be absolutely convinced they're nightmares and there's nothing you can do to change it.

But if you keep your eyes open, you'll begin to notice more is going right than you think. Look for anything that's going well, even if it's small and trivial. Perhaps they came home and shared a snack without needling each other or had a happy half-hour together on the Wii. Even if you can't spot much that's going right in their relationship, they're sure to be doing something right individually, like feeding the fish or getting out of the bath when you ask. It doesn't matter what they're doing well, it's all about noticing it and starting to see them as good guys.

We guarantee that once you start noticing the good things your children do, you'll begin to feel much more optimistic. Your children will probably notice that you're being more positive and may even start behaving better.

Praise on the spot Don't stop there – tell them you're pleased. Complimenting them helps them change their view of you, of themselves and of each other. If you aren't a natural **Cheerleader Parent**, this might not be easy either. For so many parents, being critical becomes the default mode, especially when your children are driving you mad all day:

- *'Get your fingers off the window.'*
- *'Oi! I said get your sticky fingers OFF THAT WINDOW!'*

- *'I see you poking your sister. Cut it out.'*
- *'I said CUT IT OUT! How many times do I have to tell you?'*

It's almost impossible not to notice the things your children do wrong; after all, they need to learn how to behave. But no one likes being criticized. If your boss has had a go at you, you might be grumpy when you come home and take it out on your family. If children feel constantly picked on, they can easily take it out on their siblings. So what do you do instead?

Cheerleader Parents get results by giving their children attention when they behave well and ignoring as much bad behaviour as possible.

Try appreciating them for the normal things they do:

- *'Well done putting the milk back in the fridge,'*

and also for the times they're nice to each other:

- *'Thanks for helping your brother.'*

Children love getting encouragement and reassurance that they're doing the right thing. If you can give them attention when they're behaving well, they won't always feel they need to get it by being obnoxious.

Be specific Whenever possible, the best way to praise children is to tell them exactly what they're doing right. If you gush, 'Wonderful! Aren't you amazing!', more often than not it'll go in one ear and right out the other. But if you say something kind and specific:

- *'It was really good of you to show Tina how to play Wordmole,'*
- *'I like the way you two shared that chocolate,'*
- *'Thank you for putting away your rollerblades,'*

they'll believe you mean what you say.

Praising your child for her own achievements

Be open-minded **Cheerleader Parents** recognize that every child is unique and remarkable, with her own strengths and weaknesses – they don't see one as being more talented, or another as having drawn the short straw. As they're able to see each child's individual achievements, **Cheerleader Parents**:

- Compliment their children without comparing them.
- Are careful not to judge one child by the expectations they have of another.
- Realize their children are always changing, so they don't pigeonhole or categorize them as being any particular way.

And like **Tuned-In Parents**, they:

- Don't try to make things fair by boosting one child up or squashing another down.

The result is that children of **Cheerleader Parents** feel appreciated for who they are, not in relation to their brothers and sisters. So sibling rivalry is kept to a minimum and they're more likely to help and support each other.

Cheerleader Parents don't compare their children because they know it can backfire badly. Far from encouraging your child to do what you want, comparisons can make children hate their 'perfect' siblings with an almighty passion. Brothers and sisters are different people with their own interests and abilities, who happen to be born into the same family. There's no reason to expect them to be good at the same things, so there's no point in setting up a competition between them.

If you compare them, children can easily get the impression that they're all wrong simply because they do things slightly differently.

> *My non-identical twin was always very good at maths, which my parents thought was wonderful. I was better at English.*
> *We always liked to do our homework differently. My brother came home and did his straight away. I needed a break and then tackled it after dinner. But every time my maths report came home, my parents would have a go at me. 'No wonder you didn't do so well. You could have got a better mark if you did your homework properly like he does.'*

Similarly, there's no reason to make one child feel better about her achievements by comparing her favourably to her siblings. It might be tempting to say:

- *'Aren't you clever getting your homework done. Your sister is still struggling away with hers,'*

or:

- *'Well done saying "Hello" so kindly. Your brother isn't half as polite as you are,'* or:

- *'You're wonderful getting out of bed every morning! Ben just can't seem to manage it.'*

You might be trying to motivate your child by making her feel better about herself, but comparing your children sets up an unpleasant dynamic. There's no reason why her accomplishments should be legitimized at the expense of her sibling's; she is entitled to her achievements in her own right.

Cheerleader Parents believe their children have enough competition at school. Home is so much more enjoyable for everyone if it's a place where children can explore their own interests and abilities and not feel the need to outdo each other in order to be loved and appreciated. So what can you do instead of comparing them?

It's simple: if you want to boost your child up, there's no need to mention her siblings. Instead of:

- *'If you worked as hard as your sister, you'd also be good at French,'*

try:

- *'French can be tough. You'll find it gets easier once you've spent time getting your head round that list of verbs.'*

Instead of:

- *'No wonder your brother has so many friends – he's so outgoing,'*

try:

- *'If you say hello and smile when you meet people, they realize how friendly you are.'*

Instead of:

- *'Nice goal today! I saw that great corner shot! Your brother didn't score at all!'*

try:

- 'Nice goal today! I saw that great corner shot!'

and leave the brother completely out of it.

'You keep telling me not to compare my children. But they compare themselves. What do I do?'

Siblings often compare themselves without any help from us. Some parents find it's a constant stream of:

- 'You suck at Guitar Hero. Give me the control.'
- 'I'll never be as good as Matt at the piano, so there's no point bothering.'
- 'I can't help it if you're good at football and I'm rubbish.'

Lots of children are very keen to keep up with their siblings and can learn a lot from them. But others may feel defeated if their siblings are better than they are. For some it's like a seesaw: if their sibling is clever, they must be stupid; if their sibling is attractive, they must be ugly. It's worth reminding your children that it's not a competition. Just because her brother is better at Guitar Hero doesn't mean she can't enjoy playing. More than one of them can to be good-looking, do well at school or enjoy learning a musical instrument.

Try:

- 'Let your sister have another go. She's still learning and that game takes practice.'
- 'It makes no difference if he's better at piano. Playing the piano is about learning to do something you can enjoy for the rest of your life. It has nothing to do with how well Matt plays.'
- 'It isn't about being better than your brother. It's about improving on your own terms, at your own speed.'

When children aren't evenly matched

'My son is better than his sister at almost everything. How am I supposed to compliment him without making her feel bad?'

Lots of parents worry when one child is cleverer, sportier or better looking than the other, because they don't want the less fortunate sibling to compare herself and feel unhappy about it.

If you feel sorry for the child who is younger or less talented, you might think you need to try to make things fair for her by over-praising her at the expense of her more capable sibling. But if she can see through you, she might not believe you anyway: 'You're only saying that because you're my mother.'

Also, it's not fair on her sibling. If one of your children is competent or hard-working, she's entitled to the praise she deserves. Her successes are her own and nothing to do with her sibling. You can't short-change her to spare the other one's feelings.

Instead of trying to level the playing field, try focusing on each child's individual achievements. You'll realize your less accomplished child also has all sorts of wonderful things going for her once you start looking for them. Instead of appreciating only your children's big achievements, notice the small things, because they're just as important. One child may have won a cross-country race, but the other may have worked her hardest to run a hundred metres or keep up with you on a family walk.

By noticing her little steps and efforts along the way, you'll realize the child you felt was lagging behind is doing all sorts of things you can be proud of. So even if one child is at the top of her class, you can still compliment your other one:

- 'Well done finishing your homework. I could see it was really difficult.'

It's always worth noticing how hard your children try. They may work really hard and do well, or struggle just to keep up. Either way, they like it if you notice the effort they put in.

My daughters sailed through their exams and did well. But my son is dyslexic. He's had to work like a dog, much harder than they've ever had to.

His teacher told me to keep encouraging him by complimenting all his hard work. It's really helped.

If one child is sensitive about her sibling's achievements, try giving them both lots of compliments, but in private. Making a big deal of one child so the whole family can hear can put the others off if they feel they can't measure up. If it happens a lot, they can start feeling bitter and resentful about it. So tell all your children how wonderful they are and compliment all their talents and achievements, but do it out of earshot.

My youngest started having some trouble at school. His teachers said he was lazy and not trying, but I knew it was really a confidence thing. His older siblings are all doing really well and always come home and tell me about their great marks. So I discussed it with them and they agreed to be more discreet until he's feeling a bit better about himself.

Once you start recognizing all her efforts, even your less confident child should begin to feel less jealous if her sibling is doing better than she is. As she becomes more sure of herself, it'll get much easier to praise your other child in front of her. Obviously you can continue complimenting all your children out loud for things that aren't an issue, including all the ordinary things they do, like clearing the table or picking up their toys.

When one child seems sufficiently confident already

If you have one child who is particularly gifted, you might think she's got all the confidence she needs. If she gets good exam marks and has a place on a sports team or a great part in the school play, you might even suspect she's in danger of becoming big-headed. But, underneath, she may be more insecure than you realize and still needs your approval.

My parents used to say how lucky I was because I was the oldest and tallest in my class. They said I had a huge advantage because nothing was too hard for me. My brother was the youngest in his class and they were always worrying that he wouldn't be able to keep up.

But they didn't realize I was stressed the whole time. I felt that if I slipped up, I wouldn't have any excuse for it because I was the 'lucky one'. So I worked much harder than anyone else and worried the whole time in case I did badly and everyone thought I was stupid.

They never once congratulated me because they thought it all came easily to me.

If it's obvious that your child lacks confidence, it might seem natural to give her encouragement. But if she's doing well and also seems self-assured, you may not think it's fair that she gets all the glory and you might try to make things more even between her and her siblings. But she probably minds about your opinion more than she lets on. It's far kinder to show all your children how proud of them you are.

Why we shouldn't label our children

Cheerleader Parents also try to stay open-minded. As we mentioned in Chapter 1, they know children are constantly changing, as are their interests and levels of maturity. So they try not to label anyone as the sporty one, the musical one, the sensitive one, the academic one, the sweet one or the troublemaker.

My brother was always the 'clever' one and I was always the 'sporty' one. I felt I could never be as bright as he was, but I could be good at athletics. So I trained hard, even at weekends, but never tried very hard at school.

I regret it now. We're both grown-ups and so what if I was better at sports than he was and he did better academically? I could've done pretty well at school if I'd tried.

Giving one child a title makes it their domain and it becomes very hard for another child in the family to share it. For example, if you say one of your children is the mathematical one, it implies the other isn't mathematical. When we keep banging on about one child being good at something, the others can stop trying, even though there's plenty of room for more than one artist, actor, mathematician or musician in the family.

Surprisingly, positive labels can be stifling too. We might tell a child he's the artistic one to encourage him to develop his talent, boost his confidence and let him know we've noticed he's good at something. But if we're not careful, by labelling our children when they're little we can inadvertently hold them back from developing other interests as they change and grow. They might even internalize the message that they aren't capable in other areas, and so never try. It's better to encourage all their talents and interests and keep their future paths open. Lots of things won't make sense or seem interesting until they get to secondary school, or even later. If we don't remain open-minded about our children's possibilities, they may not be open-minded either.

Furthermore, if one child doesn't seem as competent, don't treat her as the underdog or assume her siblings will always have more going for them. Children and circumstances are always changing. Your child who doesn't seem academic might go on to university and your child who doesn't seem athletic might become sporty later.

My oldest son was never any good at sports and he was always more timid and apprehensive than my other children. As a child he was too scared to go on theme-park rides and hated the wave machine at the local pool.

But when he was a teenager we took the family skiing for the first time and he was amazing. He was much better at it than all the rest of us, and wasn't scared in the slightest. He surprised us all and turned out to be a great skier.

Some parents label their children to try to get them to behave the way they'd like, by letting them know they're on to them:

- *'He's my neat child, but she's my messy one. You should see the state of her bedroom. It's like a bomb's gone off in there.'*

- 'Your brother's so helpful but you don't do anything unless I nag you.'
- 'He's polite, but this one's a cheeky little monkey.'

But these labels aren't helpful and they can so easily stick. Once your child sees himself in a particular way, it can be very difficult for him to change. And once you see your child in a particular way, it can be very hard for you to change your view of him.

Labelling your children can also build up huge resentments between you and your children, as well as between siblings.

Even when I was thirty-eight and had lived away from home for twenty years, my father was still holding on to his outdated view of me and my brother. He couldn't see we might be different people than he'd always thought. He told a neighbour, right in front of me, that my younger brother was the bright one in the family.

I couldn't believe my ears. I said, 'I've got a masters degree. I write about current affairs for a national newspaper. What more do I have to do to prove to you that I've got a brain?'

Then, trying to backtrack, he said something I found even more hurtful – that my brother was the one he could always relate to more on an intellectual level. Of course. How could I forget? The two of them have always had far more in common.

It's particularly tempting to label our children when our protective instincts have been aroused. It's easy to cast one as the victim, the sweet little angel, and the other as the aggressor, the bully, the nasty one. You might feel you need to watch the latter like a hawk for further signs of trouble. If the behaviour carries on, it can become very hard to see her as anything different. Then you don't even notice when she's nice to her siblings or when the 'victim' intentionally winds her up.

If you label one child as the bully and she internalizes the message that she's mean and horrible, it can also become a self-fulfilling prophecy. If her siblings know how you feel, they can start assuming the worst of her too, and she can get very angry about it. The angrier she gets the more resentful she feels, and before you know it she's taking it out on them.

So if you don't want your child to be a bully, don't label her as one. Every child is almost certain to go through a patch of being horrendous to her siblings. In fact, expect it. In time, the child you thought was your angel will probably get her own back.

Being labelled the 'good' child isn't as much fun as it sounds either. If one child feels locked into being good, there's never the chance to swap. She never gets to be bad and the others don't get the chance to be good. Every child deserves to make mistakes and see what happens when they behave terribly, just as every child deserves to see how it feels to get things right.

Cheerleader Parents, who don't label their children, often find one will be badly behaved for a while and then they'll swap over. It's as though the naughty one passes the baton, another child picks it up and becomes badly behaved in turn. But it isn't just parents who put children into family roles – siblings can do it to each other.

> My brother and I shared a bedroom for fifteen years and we couldn't stand each other. He was always up to something, skipping school and climbing out of the window at night. I was always well behaved and hard-working. He was determined to be totally different from me.
> Once we left home, he realized how stupid this was. Now he's become Mr Reliable, the bank manager.

In some families, stories and jokes can be brought up over and over again and used as a way of needling one sibling and keeping her in her place. Sometimes these little anecdotes are funny; they're a nice reminder of everyone's shared experiences and memories. But if the stories are meant to embarrass or perpetuate unkind labels in the family, they can become a form of group bullying.

> One Christmas, when I was little, the goldfish pond froze over and we were poking the thin ice with our feet to make holes in it. But I over-balanced and landed up to my waist in freezing-cold, muddy water. I wasn't in danger, but I felt completely humiliated. The others wouldn't stop talking about how clumsy I'd been.
> For years, if I ever slipped over, fell off my bike or broke a glass,

all my brothers would whoop with laughter, tease me and remind me, yet again, about the time I fell into the pond.

The good news is that if you don't label your children, there's less chance of this type of family culture developing. But if your children label each other anyway, see Chapter 5 on encouraging them to be nice to each other.

Can you give children too much praise?

Parents used to worry that their children would become big-headed if they complimented them too much. Nowadays parents are more likely to think that praise can help them be more confident. It can also encourage good behaviour. Instead of reinforcing the times when they're annoying pains in the neck who can't get on, it's better to encourage them to think of themselves as decent human beings who do. By praising them when they're nice to their siblings, they're likely to be kind more often.

Some children are resistant and defensive when you try to praise them and it can be very tempting to give up. But persevere if you can. Try acknowledging something they're doing right with a smile.

'My child keeps going on about how wonderful she is. She certainly doesn't need any more compliments.'

It can be embarrassing and off-putting when a child boasts about her amazing attributes and achievements. The last thing you may feel like doing is giving her more praise; in fact, you may be desperate to shut her up. But what's likely to be going on here is that she's not as sure of herself as she seems and desperately wants to be appreciated.

This is another time when it's worth remembering the Mexican finger trap: it'll probably work better if you go towards the problem instead of backing away from it. Agree with her and tell her you're proud of her. Also, try noticing the good things she does before she even mentions them. She's made it clear how much she wants approval, so go for it. Once her longing for attention is satisfied, she'll probably stop bragging. If she feels more confident on the inside, she probably won't need to keep coming to you, or anyone else, to validate her.

If she still carries on boasting and it's putting other people off, try having a quiet word with her. Explain that boasting makes other people feel uncomfortable. If she knows you're her champion and think she's completely wonderful, she may stop.

Physical Ways to Improve Your Relationship

Try being a PHYSICAL PARENT

Get them moving, feed them well and get them to bed
Physical Parents realize that children can be grumpy or hyper-sensitive if they're overtired, over-sugared, under-exercized or hungry. So they make sure their children get plenty of exercise and good food, and go to bed at a reasonable hour. They know that if their children feel well, they're far more likely to get along with everybody.

Just be there One of the best ways to improve your relationship with your child is to show that you're interested in her life. You don't necessarily have to do much of anything. Just sitting in the same room with her is a wonderful start. If you can spend time together doing the things she enjoys, like watching a video, chatting about her favourite singer or making a point of being at her sports matches, she'll feel more connected to you.

You might try turning off your laptop and your mobile phone and letting your children know you're available. Family meals are an obvious time to talk. You can also chat on the school run, before bed or even for five minutes every day when you fold the laundry. Lots of children like knowing you're near when they do their homework. Even if they don't say much to you, if they know you're available, they'll confide in you when they feel like it.

If you can't rely on seeing your children at ordinary times every day, it's still possible to hang out with them as long as you make the effort.

Since getting divorced I don't get to see my children every day. I don't want to lose them, so I focus on them as much as I can. I play card games and swingball with them, and even try to appreciate their terrible music in the car.

Be affectionate **Physical Parents** also know that there's no more obvious way to connect with your child and show her you love her than by holding her hand or giving her a cuddle. There are lots of opportunities to hug your children – when you first see them in the morning, when they leave for school, when they come home again and when they go to bed. If they don't want to be hugged that much, you can always smile at them and remember to say hello when you see them.

Looking After Yourself

Try being a Physical Parent

These physical tips apply to you, too. If you feel good because you exercise, eat well and sleep enough, you'll be far more pleasant to be around. You'll also be more able to put your energies into connecting with your children and better able to cope with their arguments.

But life can get so complicated and so fraught when we have more than one child that taking care of ourselves can get pushed to the bottom of the list. If you're irritable, exhausted or feeling depressed about your jelly belly, the stress of sibling rivalry is far more likely to get to you and you're more likely to overreact. So if you can, try to look after yourself as well as your children.

Try being a Laid-Back Parent

When you're feeling outnumbered and you need to make some time for yourself, accept help. There's no way you can do everything for your family, get some exercise or have your hair cut once in a blue moon without someone else looking after your children occasionally.

Building a good relationship with your children isn't just about slogging on and on to try to make things better. Sometimes you're better off taking a break. Let someone else take them to the park every now and again, or swap children with another mother to give both of you some time off. The better you feel, the easier it will be to cope with family life.

Building Your Child's Confidence

The better your child feels about herself, the less likely she is to project her insecurities and frustrations on to you or her siblings. Confident children don't need to put other people down to make themselves feel better.

Try being a Pause Parent

You can't help her become more confident if she feels picked on and persecuted. So when you have the urge to be critical, pause and zip your lip.

Try being a Cheerleader Parent

Instead, give her specific compliments so she'll believe what you say. The way you see her affects the way she sees herself.

Try being a Tuned-In Parent

Your child will feel more loved and secure if she believes you understand her and think she's a good person.

Try being a Commando Parent

Once you've listened, you can give her straightforward advice and help her put her feelings into perspective.

Try being a Physical Parent
How she feels physically will affect how confident she feels emotionally. So help her to get plenty of sleep, exercise and healthy food.

Try being a Sorted Parent
She can gain confidence if you tell her what to expect ahead of time and show her that, by practising, she can get better at almost anything.

Try being a Laid-Back Parent
When she's ready, allow her to do more. She'll feel good about herself knowing you believe in her and have faith that she'll do the right thing.

Encourage Your Child to Take Responsibility
Try being a LAID-BACK PARENT

Allow them to do more **Laid-Back Parents** boost their relationship with their children by showing them how much they trust them to do the right thing. They have faith that their children have good ideas and can make good decisions. They also know that, in general, the more confident children feel, the nicer they'll be.

A great way to start is to allow your children to do more for themselves. Obviously this should be related to their age and level of maturity, but suggestions include letting your toddler choose her own clothes, allowing your eight-year-old to help you cook or letting your pre-teen make short trips on her own.

My mother-in-law was very neurotic. She always had a reason why my husband wasn't capable of doing anything around the house.
I'm the opposite: I try to let my children do everything. They sit

with me in the kitchen chopping up fruit and vegetables. My two-year-old is only slicing bananas with a blunt table knife, but it's a start. We make jam, plant flowers in the garden, we even painted the bedrooms over Easter. They love it and so do I. We have a great time together.

My husband says that at the ages of two, four and five they can do more than he did when he was twelve. He also says they're much closer to me than he ever was to his mum. 🍃

Letting them do more gives them a chance to learn new skills and gives you a chance to compliment them.

It also helps your relationship if you let them make some of their own decisions.

🍃 *I argued with my mother for years because she kept insisting I should wear a vest. If she'd had her way, I would have worn a vest every day of my life. It was such a stupid thing to fight about and such a waste of time.*

I try not to get into the same silly arguments with my children. If they don't want to wear a vest or a coat, that's their decision. If they get cold they might decide to put one on next time. 🍃

Though spending a lot of time with your children like a **Physical Parent** is a good way to strengthen your relationship, they may also appreciate the times you're a **Laid-Back Parent** and step back. They'll be pleased that you have faith in them.

🍃 *My mother trusted me to go out for hours on my bicycle. She was right – I was careful and never had a problem, and I loved the freedom.*

When I was older, in my gap year before university, I wanted to go to India on my own and she let me. I was happy about it then, and I'm happy now when I remember how much confidence she had in me. I'll always be grateful to her for trusting me. 🍃

Sort Out Problems Before They Arise

Try being a SORTED PARENT

Sort your systems **Sorted Parents** help their children feel secure because they're organized and reliable. Children are happier when systems are in place because they know what behaviour is acceptable and what isn't, and what will happen if the rules aren't followed.

Being sorted can get rid of a lot of ambiguity, which can cause children to feel resentful towards you and their siblings. As we've mentioned, lots of parents find they punish one child, but come up with myriad excuses why it's OK for another child to do the same thing and get away with it. They may not even realize they're doing it. When children can't trust you to be impartial, they can be on constant alert, looking out for tiny inconsistencies. When they notice them, they can take it personally, and if they believe that you're favouring their sibling, animosity can start building up.

Set up rules Instead of making up rules and consequences on the spot, **Sorted Parents** organize them ahead of time. Because they've thought them through, children don't have to worry that one sibling is getting a better deal.

So instead of coming up with punishments on the spot:

- *'You hit your sister because she called you names? Go to your room and don't even think you are going to that birthday party tomorrow,'*

try being clear what the rules and punishments are in advance:

- *'From now on, anyone who calls names gets fifteen minutes' time out, and anyone who hits gets an hour.'*

If you set things up this way, they're less likely to think that you're biased when it's time to enforce consequences.

Give advance warning **Sorted Parents** also head off arguments by giving their children advance warning about the behaviour they expect, long before they start winding each other up again.

- *Just to let you know, if there's any more fighting when we get to the café, we'll have to go home. Other people don't want to listen to you quarrelling with each other.*

By talking to your children ahead of time, you can be reasonable about it. This is better for your relationship than overreacting when the same old thing happens again.

Take Charge!
Try being a COMMANDO PARENT

Commando Parents are great at providing a stable home, and their children feel very safe and secure knowing their parents are in charge. In lots of ways they're like good teachers, who somehow manage to control quantities of children just by raising an eyebrow.

When I was at school, my favourite teachers were firm but fair. When they came into the room, the whole class settled down and behaved. When less assertive teachers took the lessons, we all hated it. There was so much noise and time-wasting. There was one boy, Dean, who used to shout and whirl bookbags around. They couldn't manage him, and I found it really frightening.

At home, I'm quite firm because I want my children to feel safe and know I have things under control.

Even when there's a problem, natural **Commandos** aren't knocked off balance. They know it's reassuring for everyone when they're in charge. Their children tend to have faith in them, even when they're adults themselves.

Whenever my mum comes to visit, I breathe a sigh of relief. She takes over and I know everything is going to be fine.

Being able to be authoritative while maintaining a decent

relationship with your children is a good thing for everybody. If you can keep a calm atmosphere in the house, you can say goodbye to lots of arguments that put everyone on edge. Without the unnecessary anxiety and fear, you'll find your children treat each other better.

But if you're not naturally assertive and don't feel things are under control, this might seem like a long way off. So next we'll show you how to get cooperation without stirring up any more animosity or compromising your relationship with your children.

How to Be in Charge without Alienating Your Children

In any family there are things that need to be done, and you're the one who has to make them happen. But if one or more of your children isn't cooperative and you have to plead, shout or worse to get them moving, it can be a classic cause of friction between you. If you're not a natural **Commando**, you can even find you're making things worse.

- If you have to nag one child over and over again to get dressed, behave at the table or whatever, she can feel you're picking on her and resent you for it. She can take up a lot of your time, and if your cooperative children feel they're being ignored or taken for granted, they can get resentful too.

- If one child is difficult, sometimes it's easier to give up altogether, rather than insist she does what she's told or pulls her weight around the house. But if your other children notice she's getting away with it, they're likely to feel aggrieved.

- If you have to shout like a banshee to get any of your children to cooperate, you'll end up angry and exhausted. On bad days, even mundane things like getting them to brush their teeth can become a major production. This is not only annoying and a big waste of time, it can affect all the relationships in the house. When there's a lot of aggro, everyone is more likely to be on edge and turn on each other.

It would be so nice to get to the point where all your children will cooperate without a fuss. If they don't waste time arguing about things that have to be done anyway, you won't need to nag them and you'll have more time to do the things that you all enjoy.

So how do you get cooperation without straining the relationships in your house? The good news is that if you've been trying any of our suggestions in this chapter, especially pausing, praising and tuning in, your children may already be quite receptive. If they feel connected to you, they're more likely to do what you say, simply because you can have a reasonable conversation about it. Try being a:

- **Sorted Parent** – take time to set up rules in advance.
- **Laid-Back Parent** – encourage your children to want to do the right thing.
- **Commando Parent** – tell them what needs to be done and why it's important to you.

If these aren't working, you can also try tuning in further and finding out if there's a reason they aren't cooperating.

Try being a SORTED PARENT

Give advance warning and set up rules **Sorted Parents** very seldom get to the out-of-control-shouting stage. So how do they get their family to cooperate? By giving their children as much advance warning as possible when they need something done.

There are probably some seriously **Sorted Parents** who can anticipate problems before they happen in the first place, and we're in awe of them. Before there's even a hint of trouble they might say:

- *'You can play until six thirty, but then we all need to tidy up.'*

They know this works much better than swooping in with no warning while their children are having fun, parcelling out chores and shouting at them.

But for the rest of us, it's enough to be able to sort out a problem before it happens again. Try telling each child exactly what you expect them to do and then remind them two or three times about the plan. They might grumble, but they'll probably take it in. When the crunch comes, you might be amazed how little resistance and back chat you get.

Try being a LAID-BACK PARENT

Ask the family for ideas **Laid-Back Parents** don't often get to the shouting stage either, and they're also good at getting their children to cooperate. They do it by asking them for ideas so that they feel included and want to do the right thing.

- *'You two fight over the basin and the mirror every morning. What can you do about it?'*

Laid-Back Parents ask for solutions because they know how well it works. Children are usually flattered to be asked, and they're far more likely to follow through with ideas if they've come up with them in the first place.

Get help **Laid-Back** types go in with the attitude that their children are capable of making a contribution. They know that when they're overstretched they don't have much energy left to be kind. So they make sure that everyone helps out.

There might be all sorts of reasons why you treat your children differently (see pages 92–9), but if one child keeps getting away with doing less than the others, you aren't really doing her any favours. If she doesn't know how to tidy a bedroom, work a washing machine or motivate herself when she doesn't want to do something, it's not good for her in the long run.

If she also feels entitled to let her siblings take the strain, they'll resent her for it. Or if she expects you to do everything, you might set out to be the perfect nurturing parent but get tired and end up snapping at her anyway. If one child is getting a better deal than the others or you're doing too much for her, the first thing is to admit it to yourself. If you change your approach mentally, you should find it easier to be firm when you want them all to make a contribution.

Every Saturday since we were small, my brother and I were expected to help Dad wash his car. We enjoyed sloshing water around so much that eventually we did the neighbours' cars too. We had loads of fun and we earned quite a lot of pocket money.

They might even find they enjoy it and start working together as a team. But if your children still won't cooperate, it's time to be a **Commando**.

Try being a COMMANDO PARENT

Natural **Commandos** know that it's possible to be in charge without spinning out of control. Strengthening your authority doesn't mean roaring and raging at your children – which can frighten them or make them very angry so that, instead of cooperating, they argue back or try not to spend any time with you.

My mother was a very powerful person, and she was definitely the boss in our family. She ordered us all around. If we ever dared to mis-behave she'd shout, and even hit us. There was so much tension at home that none of us ever wanted to be there.

So what can you do instead? As we've mentioned, preparation is key: if you can remember to give advance warning or ask your children for ideas, they'll know what's supposed to be happening and you might not have to get heavy about it. Here are some **Commando** skills that can also help.

Give orders that don't sound like orders **Commando Parents** have an incredible knack of giving clear instructions without getting their children's backs up. You'll find this is particularly useful for bolshie children who tend to argue back if you give them a direct command.

Orders That Don't Sound Like Orders

Here is a quick recap – see Chapter 1 for more detail.

Give options *'You could do your teeth now or let your sister use the bathroom first.'* This cleverly bypasses the whole argument about whether it's time to get ready for bed.

Say it in a word *'Dishwasher.'* If your child already knows it's her turn to empty it, there's no need to annoy her with a long explanation.

Describe what you see *'The hamster cage needs cleaning.'* Say it in a neutral voice and let her work out the next step.

Ask what comes next *'You've finished your snack – what's next?'* They know it's time for homework. They've done it every day at this time for years.

Give a quick reminder *'Remember to share.'* This is much more positive than *'You're so selfish.'*

Whisper *'Tissue?'* Useful technique when one of your children is picking her nose in public.

Give thanks in advance *'Thanks for keeping your music down while your sister's doing her homework.'* If you're lucky, she might think she meant to do it anyway.

Write a note *'Flush the loo!'* When something is written down, children often take it more seriously.

Express your feelings Another good way to get things done is to tell your children how you feel. This can also work much better than giving them direct orders.

Instead of:

* *'Just be QUIET!'*

try:

* *'It's embarrassing when I'm on the telephone and you two are arguing.'*

This isn't about laying a guilt-trip on them, but telling them what the problem is.

> ❛ *I told my children how much I minded finding their clean clothes dumped on the floor of their bedroom after I had spent ages ironing and folding them. Then they surprised me. They looked right at me and apologized, folded up the clothes and put them away properly.* ❜

By sticking to the format *'I feel . . .'* rather than *'You always . . .'* you're giving them a chance to do the right thing.

Expressing your feelings is a good way to communicate with the adults as well as the children in your family.

> ❛ *If my husband starts ordering me around, it gets my blood up and I'll argue back. But if he tells me how he feels, I'll go out of my way to help him.*
>
> *My kids are just the same. If I tell them why I'm upset or why I really want something done, they'll often do what they can.* ❜

Use consequences It's not great for your authority if you snap out punishments, especially the kind you have no intention of enforcing.

So instead of:

* *'I CAN'T STAND you two fighting over that tricycle any more. I'm giving it AWAY!'*

try:

- *'If you're not going to be reasonable, I'll have to put the tricycle away, and you can both find something else to play with.'*

The first approach might get you a round of shrieks and wails, and isn't great for your relationship. If you then backtrack because you feel guilty, it's not going to help your authority either.

You aren't going to win any popularity contests by using the second approach and sticking to it either. But if all your children know what to expect, when you enforce consequences it's usually a much calmer affair. You've thought things through, you've told them the plan and you'll feel more quietly confident about standing up for yourself without shouting.

It's very helpful for children to know there will be repercussions for the things they do and don't do. It's part of learning how to become a reasonable human being. If possible, the consequences should relate to the crime. Try:

- *'You've knocked your brother's drink over. Please wipe it up.'*
- *'If you two don't get ready for bed now, there won't be time for a story.'*
- *'If you don't help me clear up, I won't feel like helping you next time you ask me for a favour.'*

It's better to talk through consequences in advance so that you don't have to be a dragon to enforce them. But even if you haven't been that organized, it's not a disaster. As long as you're clear in your own mind that the repercussions are reasonable, you'll usually have enough authority in your voice to make them work. Another bonus about being reasonable is that if each of your children understands *why* you're insisting on certain rules, they're less likely to feel you're picking on them.

If you're not a natural **Commando** and one child is particularly tricky, you might worry that being honest and straightforward is only going to lead to trouble.

My relationship with my son is quite shaky, so I stay away from awkward subjects. I don't want to risk going two steps forward, three steps back with him.

But there are times when we have to be assertive with difficult children. For the sake of everyone in the family, there are things they have to do and it's up to us to tell them. Being a **Commando** isn't going to threaten your relationship if you're also doing lots of tuning in and praising. Even if they defy you and you feel as though you're going backwards, keep persevering and you'll get there in the end.

For the moment, if you find you're getting into a stalemate, your best option is to . . .

Try being a TUNED-IN PARENT

When being tough isn't working, it's worth finding out what's going on underneath. Often children behave unreasonably and refuse to cooperate because they have strong feelings about something. Listening will help melt their resistance and can help get you out of sticky situations.

My children broke a glass jug. I wasn't angry, but I insisted they had to clear it up. I told them to collect the pieces and wrap them in newspaper, hoover up the bits and wipe the floor.

One of them wouldn't help. She kept saying she was busy, and I was getting more and more annoyed with her. Finally she admitted that she didn't really know how to wrap up the glass and she was worried about cutting her hands. Once I understood, I showed her how to do it and she worked very hard to help her brother clean it up properly.

If you need a refresher course on tuning in, there's a lot more about it earlier in this chapter. As we mentioned before, it is probably the most important way to open the lines of communication between you and your children and build a good relationship between you.

All your efforts to build a better relationship with your children will cut down on jealousy, competitiveness and resentment. You'll find this will also improve your children's relationship and they'll have much less to quarrel about. Even if fights do break out, you'll be in a better position to intervene because your children will be more likely to listen to you. In the next chapter we'll show you what you can do to stop an argument.

4

How to Stop an Argument
Four Strategies That Really Work

So, here's the sixty-four-million-dollar question. Your children are fighting (again), things are going downhill and you want them to cut it out. How on earth do you get them to stop? If you can resist the urge to strangle them all, you've got four good options. You can:

- **Ask your children how to solve it**

If you're a natural **Laid-Back Parent**, you'll know one of the simplest ways to stop an argument is to ask your children for the solution. When they come up with the answer, they're far more likely to stick to it.

- **Choose not to get sucked in**

If you're a natural **Pause Parent**, you'll know how effective it can be to stay out of sibling squabbles altogether. When your children know that bickering won't get your attention, they'll often stop on their own.

- **Get tough and make them stop**

If you're a natural **Commando Parent**, you'll know that a swift, firm intervention can nip trouble in the bud. When the situation is already horrible and you can't stand any more noise and aggravation, this can also be a quick, efficient way of ending it.

- **Calm things down**

If you're a naturally **Tuned-In Parent**, you'll know that you can defuse lots of arguments by listening to everyone's feelings. When each child gets to air his grievances and knows you'll listen, they'll often stop fighting.

All four can help you to stop your children's arguments in their tracks, and we'll talk you through each of them.

Ask Your Children How to Solve It

One of the easiest, most effective ways to stop an argument is to ask your children to solve the problem themselves. We came across this nugget when we asked children what their parents should do when they quarrel. One child told us, 'They should just ask US for ideas. We know why we're fighting.'

Even if you feel your children can't possibly solve it because they're too young or the issue is too complicated, it's worth letting them have a shot at it. It's great to encourage our children to think for themselves and they'll appreciate the chance to try. It can be very liberating for them to come up with the answers and it's surprising how good their ideas can be.

Asking your children for solutions is also a wonderful alternative from a parent's perspective. Children often have clarity where we don't. You may find they have simple, straightforward answers to complex problems.

My children were having yet another argument, and the accusations were so complicated I couldn't keep up. In desperation, I tried asking them what to do about it. They said they should just stop hitting each other. And they did. The argument stopped completely.

And there I was thinking they were punching each other because one called the other an idiot, because the other stole the TV control, because the first turned the sound up too loud, because, because, because. It was such a relief not to have to unravel that one.

It doesn't matter what solution your children suggest, as long as you're all happy with it. Plus they'll be more keen to make it work and more likely to stick to it if it's their own idea. If you'd suggested the same thing yourself, they'd probably refuse to do it!

When your children successfully solve their problems, you'll feel great about your amazing super-parent skills. You'll realize you're capable of changing the dynamic, and turning angry, grumbling children into cheerful playmates and rational people.

Trying this approach may even stop them getting into so many arguments in the future. If they can reach an agreement a number of times, they might begin to realize they don't need to get so worked up when their siblings annoy them. Instead of reacting (or overreacting) over and over again, they may start thinking, 'What can we do about this one?' You might even overhear them working through an issue all on their own that previously would have led to a full-scale row.

How to Do It

Try being a LAID-BACK PARENT

Ask for solutions Asking your children for the answer can be one of the easiest ways to stop a fight. If you haven't tried it before, give it a go. If you want to be subtle, try:

- *'Can you two work this out, or do you need my help?'*

It plants the idea that they can start resolving things on their own. If this doesn't work, you can be more straightforward:

- *'How do you think you could solve this?'*

If they come up with an answer, you get the opportunity to compliment them and tell them how good they are at negotiating, listening, sharing or understanding. The next time they have a problem, you can remind them how clever they were:

- *'I know you two can work this out. Like the other day when you both wanted cornflakes and the packet was almost empty, but you decided to split what was left.'*

You're telling them you have confidence in them and giving them the evidence to back it up. With any luck they'll think:

- 'Yes, we are good at sorting out problems and Mum wants to know how we'd get round this one. Well how about . . .'

You may already be asking your children for solutions without even realizing it.

💧 *I discovered by accident that sometimes it's better to get my children to resolve their own problems. My daughter said something snide to her brother and he lost his temper and hurled a ruler at her head. She burst into tears and ran out of the room.*

I was so shocked I could hardly speak. I managed to blurt out, 'I'm too angry even to talk to you. Sort this out with her NOW!' and I left.

Ten minutes later I found them upstairs together. They were sitting on her bed, both smiling, and he had his arm around her. They both looked fine.

They didn't want any advice or input from me and asked me politely to go away. They said they were getting on just fine on their own. 💧

If you've never tried asking your children to solve their own quarrels, you'll be pleased how many good ideas they have and how capable they are.

But It's Not Working . . .

'I'm so annoyed! My children started solving all sorts of problems on their own, but it didn't last. Now they're right back to fighting again.'

Once they get the hang of it, it's tempting to get overconfident and think you can leave it all up to your children. But there are still going to be times when they'll need you there to arbitrate. They'll need more experience and maturity before they can sort out everything on their own.

'Asking my children for solutions sounded such a great idea. But when I tried it, they refused to cooperate.'
If your children won't stop arguing, won't come up with a compromise, or if they just stand there looking at you blankly, you may need to do some more work behind the scenes to encourage them to come up with ideas.

In lots of ways, asking your children how to solve their problems is similar to having a family brainstorming session, which we cover in depth in Chapter 5. The main difference is that you can ask them for solutions immediately rather than setting up a formal meeting. But the resistance and difficulties you're likely to encounter are pretty much the same. So if it isn't working for you, see pages 174–85.

It's also worth remembering there are three other great things you can do to stop an argument, and we'll talk you through each of them.

Choose Not to Get Sucked In

Pause Parents know that if their children are in the middle of a stupid little disagreement, it's often better not to get involved at all. Though it's incredibly annoying when your children are trading insults, if you can block out 90 per cent of it and act as though none of it is happening, they'll often get bored and stop. If you don't jump in, you're also giving them another chance to work things out on their own.

Keeping quiet, blocking your ears or going into another room isn't always as easy as it sounds. If you're used to intervening at the faintest hint of trouble or unkindness, it's hard to hold back. Or you might start off by ignoring low-level bickering, then explode anyway when it gets to you. There are also going to be times when you can't ignore your children's arguments; if things are spiralling out of control or they really need your help, you can't stay detached.

But there are so many situations when staying out of the fight is your best option. If you suspect much of their discord is attention-seeking, getting perpetually dragged in isn't going to help and might just exacerbate it. If you micro-manage everything your children do and say to each other, you'll drive them crazy and they'll be missing out on the opportunity to learn how to solve things themselves. Furthermore, if you react immediately, you can easily say and do things you regret. Holding back and keeping a clear head can be much more effective.

Here's how to stop getting sucked into all your children's disagreements and what to do if they keep arguing anyway.

How to Do It
Try being a PAUSE PARENT

Zip your lip Start by deciding to do things differently. Tell yourself that you don't actually have to get involved every time your children disagree and it's often better if you don't. Try staying quiet just to see what happens. The situation may not be as bad as you think and your children might even sort themselves out without you.

> We were on the motorway and my youngest was playing with an annoying squeaky keyring. My oldest suddenly burst out, 'If you don't stop making that noise, I'll throw that thing out of the window!' My hands tightened on the steering wheel and I suspected we were in for trouble: a big fight, followed by tears.
>
> I was about to intervene, when my youngest laughed. He wasn't fazed at all. 'If you do that, I'll throw your iPhone out of the window.'
>
> My oldest laughed too. 'Then I'll throw YOU out of the window.'
>
> 'Ha!' said the little one. 'Then the policeman will throw YOU into jail.' They both laughed again. I couldn't believe it – they were enjoying themselves.

Of course there are going to be times when you won't be so lucky. Instead of going into a comedy routine, they might start punching each other and then, of course, you'll have to intervene. But by staying quiet and listening, you're leaving the possibility open for your children to work things out. Also, you're not inadvertently turning an everyday situation into something stressful, or making a bad situation worse by misjudging it.

> *I had a hell of a morning. When I came into the kitchen my daughter was yelling at my son, and I yelled at her too for picking on him. But I didn't have the full story.*
>
> *Last night my daughter tried to use our electric bread-maker. But it didn't work, and this morning he was teasing her about the nasty doughy lump she'd baked.*
>
> *I wish I'd never interfered because I made everything ten times worse. My daughter was so upset when she left for school she didn't say goodbye and she slammed the door behind her. I've been feeling guilty about it all day.*

However tempting it is to get involved, try being a **Pause Parent** and resist the urge to dive into the fray. Despite your good intentions, it's so easy to get stressed and then whip everyone up into a frenzy. One child we know told his mother:

> *Mum, if you're not calm, you aggravate the whole situation. If you're angry we get angry too. You affect how we feel.*

So instead, do whatever it takes to stay quiet, say nothing and see what happens. You never know – your children might surprise you and stop arguing.

Calm down fast If you aren't a natural **Pause Parent**, you might find it hard to stay calm because the slightest hint of aggression sets your nerves on edge. Lots of parents are wired up this way: loud noises, rude voices or general low-level niggling send their blood pressure and adrenaline sky-rocketing.

Others get stressed because they were brought up to believe that sibling arguments are wrong or dangerous. If you recognize yourself here, of course you don't want your children to hurt or hate each other, but not all disagreements are damaging. If you quash every little hint of trouble, your children miss the chance to learn all sorts of important life skills, like negotiating and sticking up for themselves.

If you notice you're getting anxious or angry and the situation doesn't necessarily warrant it, concentrate on calming down. Take a few deep breaths, walk out of the room or get a glass of water. Give yourself a chance to think things through and come back later. Even if the situation goes unexpectedly downhill, you haven't lost anything because you'll probably be a lot more effective.

Why It's Important to Feel In Control

According to psychologists, people find situations particularly stressful when they have very little control over them. Parents are no exception. Pausing doesn't mean sitting there against your will, gritting your teeth, wishing you had some earplugs and a large bottle of wine to drown out the noise. It makes all the difference if you can make a conscious decision:

- Not to get involved
- To stay quiet and zip your lip
- To walk out of the room to do some deep breathing

Don't worry if you can't: we'll show you other options later.

Keep things in perspective and wait until later Some parents find it so distressing when their children fight that they get into a tailspin and feel their whole family life is spiralling out of control. But even if you're feeling all churned up and can't see what to do immediately, there's no need to panic. You're doing something positive by staying quiet and you're not expected to solve everything immediately.

If everyone is upset, they may not listen to you anyway. Sometimes it's better to discuss the problem when they're all feeling more rational. If necessary, walk away or wait for your children to calm down and resolve the issue later.

Expect to get wound up You may not be consciously aware that you react (or overreact) every time your children fight. But if you do, they can get into the habit of bickering simply to get your attention. They may try all sorts of tactics to rope you in: teasing each other, snatching possessions, bopping each other on the head, all to get you to notice. If this is the case, the more you respond to the fighting, the more they'll do it.

The only way to break this particularly irritating cycle is to be aware of it. Then you'll be in a far better position to contain yourself.

I read a parenting book that told me to ignore my children when they were fighting, and I thought the advice was stupid. It's my job to make sure they treat each other properly.

But I seemed to be fire-fighting all day to put out their arguments, through every meal and every time we got in the car. I dreaded spending time with them.

I complained to my husband about it, but he just kept saying, 'What's the problem? They're fine with me.' I felt like strangling him.

'Fine,' I said. 'Next time it happens, YOU take over.'

At Saturday lunch the insults started again, so I pretended I had to go out on an errand. I opened and shut the front door, but stayed in the hall to listen. I couldn't believe it. No quarrelsome voices or patronizing comments. In fact, they were all chatting away quite normally. That weekend, I tried the experiment several more times and came to the humiliating conclusion that I must be part of the problem, because they don't argue when their dad's in charge.

'Why do they fight when I'm around?' I complained that night in bed.

'Because they know it gets to you,' he said smugly. 'It doesn't get to me at all, so they know there's no point.'

This mother said she still finds it hard not to react, but she is getting better at it. She continued her story:

Yesterday my son said to his sister, 'What are you doing watching television? You're a girl. You should be in the kitchen washing up.'

This is just the kind of teasing I hate, and I could feel myself getting irritated. But I decided not to say anything. They looked at each other, and then they burst out laughing. 'We were SO sure you were going to fall for that one, Mum.' Honestly!

When you can anticipate what gets to you, it's easier to prepare yourself. You might know you're likely to get stressed in the morning when you're short of time, at bedtime when you're already tired, or in the school holidays when your children are hanging around the house all day picking on each other. If you're mentally prepared for the onslaught, you're in a much better position to control yourself instead of letting it control you.

But It's Not Working . . .

'Sometimes my children wind each other up to get my attention, so I don't want to encourage them. But if I ignore them, the fighting gets worse. What can I do?'

Try being a CHEERLEADER PARENT

Notice the good, ignore the bad If your children are fighting to get your attention, it's also worth trying to be a **Cheerleader Parent**. If they want you to react, they'll keep trying all sorts of tactics to hook you in, like fighting louder, longer and harder to get you to notice them.

So try giving them lots of attention when they're *not* fighting. Make time to chat about their day at school, talk about things that interest them at the dinner table and try to make a little time to talk when you put them to bed. You could also focus on behaviour you want to encourage. Notice the times they're kind to each other and keep an eye out for anything good they do. If you can fill up the attention-seeking hole, they may cut down on some of the arguing.

Giving your children lots of positive attention is a long-term project. So for now you need to find a method of breaking up fights without giving them negative attention and undoing all your good work. You could start by beefing up your **Commando** skills to get them to stop (see pages 37–8).

'I don't get involved in their fights, but only because I don't know what the hell to do. I sit there frozen but panicking inside.'

It may not be fun, sitting there with your mouth gaping, your heart hammering and your brain on standby. But at least you aren't making the situation worse.

There are three classic stress responses, *fight*, *flight* and *freeze*, and when your children argue you may naturally go into freeze mode. Don't give yourself a hard time about it because pausing is a good option. Flight isn't a disaster either, as long as their fighting isn't too extreme; there's nothing wrong with locking yourself in the loo for five minutes to calm down. The one to worry about is the fight response, because you can easily find yourself shouting, saying terrible things, physically dragging your children apart or even smacking them.

If you freeze, you may not know what to do at the time, but when your brain thaws out things will become clear. Luckily there's plenty you can do to resolve the problem after everyone has calmed down.

'I'm leaving my children to sort out their own arguments. But how do I know they're really all right?'

By pausing we aren't suggesting you should always do nothing. Sometimes your children need your help. If you keep pausing but they're still fighting, you might need to be more proactive.

We've heard enough horror stories from traumatized adults and children to know that you definitely can't ignore everything. One or more of your children may be putting up with more than you realize, and if you don't take action and help him out, he can suffer and feel profoundly let down.

My older sister bullied me a lot and my parents didn't seem to notice. I knew it wasn't right, but I didn't feel I could ask for help. I knew that if I told anyone, she'd find a way to get me back by being even more spiteful. So I just held it all inside.

What was my mother doing all those years? Did she know what was going on, or just pretend it wasn't happening? Maybe she was too busy to notice or felt I should stand up for myself. Now it's too late, so I'll never know.

It's a shame because I went through years of fear and misery, and it needn't have been that way.

Even children who seem to be evenly matched or quite tough may need more help than you think.

My older brother and I fought for years. It was physical stuff – punching, kicking and shoving. I gave him as good as I got. But looking back, I wonder why my parents never did anything about it. They never asked if we needed help; we had to handle everything on our own. I remember once I went to my mother because he'd given me a bloody nose, and she told me to stop crying and get on with it.

So what can you do?

Try being a TUNED-IN PARENT

Listen to their feelings Even if your children can usually resolve their differences and seem to be managing all right without you, don't just assume they're fine. Though they may seem to be able to resolve some arguments on their own, it's a good idea to check how each of them feels afterwards. If you try to keep your tone light and don't interrogate them, they're more likely to tell you how they feel. Try variations of:

- 'She sounded pretty angry with you. You probably felt the same about her.'
- 'That sounded like quite an argument. What happened in the end?'

- *'You two have been very quiet since tea. Are you speaking to each other?'*
- *'So were you happy with the way everything got divided out?'*

Most importantly, let your children know that, though you're happy that they can solve their own problems, they can come to you if they need you:

- *'It was great the way you two worked things out today. But if you ever need to, come and find me. I'll always listen and help if I can.'*

Get Tough and Make Them Stop

Asking your children for solutions or choosing not to get involved can be helpful, but they're not the answer to every sibling argument. Your third option is to get tough and make your children stop.

Some parents are great at nipping trouble in the bud. When their children start flicking peas at each other, they jump right in with, 'That's enough. Whoever flicks the next pea is leaving the table.' They look and sound as if they mean business, and their children start behaving.

If you're good at it, being firm can be quick and effective. It works best to act immediately, long before the pea-flicking escalates into insults, kicks or a volley of flying vegetables. By stepping in before anyone has had a chance to get really wound up, minor incidents don't turn into major problems. If the situation is already spiralling out of control or looking dangerous, it's even more important to take action.

But if getting tough always worked the way you planned (be honest here), would you have picked up this book? You may already know that intervening isn't always easy and that you can inadvertently make the situation worse.

You might find yourself pleading, 'Come on – please cut it out. Please . . .' while they ignore you. You might repeat what you said, but louder, 'I said CUT THAT OUT NOW!' And when that doesn't work? Your blood pressure soars, you lose your temper and you threaten hideous consequences. Eventually your children might start behaving, but they'll be resentful, and you can feel stressed and guilty for hours. Whether you need a bit more authority (less pleading) or a bit more restraint (less shouting), we'll talk you through it.

How to Do It
Try being a COMMANDO PARENT

If the fighting isn't serious, a short, firm intervention can be a great option. When it works, it can prevent mundane bickering from escalating into something much worse. For natural **Commandos** it's no big deal to tell their children to stop fighting, take it elsewhere, or set consequences if they carry on. That's it. Problem solved.

We're not talking about the shouters; it's the people who have natural authority who are amazing. To the rest of us, it can seem nothing short of miraculous.

> *I was having a cup of coffee with my neighbour. Suddenly there was a lot of noise and her children came running in complaining.*
>
> *'He snatched the Gameboy!'*
>
> *'But it's MY Gameboy. He shouldn't have been using it!'*
>
> *'Thank you,' she said calmly. 'You know the rule. We don't snatch toys from people. As I'm busy right now, I'll put it up on this shelf and we'll discuss this later.'*
>
> *They handed it over without another word, she put it out of reach and we carried on with our coffee. I couldn't believe what I saw. That would have led to World War III at my house.*
>
> *A week later I saw her again. 'What happened about the Gameboy?' I asked. She looked puzzled. 'Oh. I forgot all about it and so did they. I guess it's still up there.'*

The annoying thing is that grandparents and nannies often

have a lot more authority than parents, because they can be firm without getting stressed or emotional about it.

I did a Tesco run on the way home from work and was putting the bags away while our nanny gave the children their tea. She's a tiny little thing, only five foot, but she's amazing.

At the table, the two boys started teasing my daughter and being mean. I thought, 'Oh no, here we go. There's going to be a big scene.' But our nanny wasn't so easily discouraged.

'That's not nice,' she said firmly. 'You need to apologize to Ella.'

My oldest apologized straight away. She gave the other one a beady look. 'Sorry Ella,' he mumbled. That was the end of it.

If you're not a natural **Commando**, life's not so simple. You might start off well:

- *'Hey, stop that.'*
- *'I'll have that toy until you decide how to share it.'*
- *'That's enough. You need to say sorry.'*

However hard you try to be the calm figure of authority, if the fighting gets to you, you can still snap. Suddenly you're embroiled in the tangle, inadvertently making things worse.

When it's all too much, I lose it. But what else can I do? I ask them to stop provoking each other, but two minutes later they're back at it. So I shout. I try to separate them physically. I threaten terrible consequences and I shout louder.

Every weekend I think we're going to have a happy family time. But if they bicker and I overreact, the entire weekend is ruined.

When all those parenting experts go on about being consistent, this is often what they mean. If you threaten punishments and don't stick to them, your children will know from experience that you don't necessarily mean what you say.

Even if they're doing something mindless like watching TV, my children can find something to argue about. Yesterday, one went to the bathroom and the other stole his favourite chair, claiming that it was his turn to have it. They ended up in a huge row. I couldn't take it any more, so I swore at them to stop and told them they were both banned from all screens for a month.

They're still not speaking to each other, and neither of them will speak to me.

This mother told us later that she didn't have the heart to stick to the screen ban.

I felt so guilty about shouting and swearing, and I couldn't bear the fact that no one was talking. I cracked after two days just to restore some peace. Now the TV and computers and everything else are back on. But I'm still not feeling great about it.

If this sounds like you, don't give up. It's possible to stop the fighting without going ballistic or losing your authority. Here's how.

Give orders that don't sound like orders Though **Commando Parents** can be tough, instead of going straight into a difficult situation barking orders, they're usually more subtle. They might start by making it clear what has to be done and then leave it up to their children to do the right thing.

Orders That Don't Sound Like Orders

Here's another quick recap:

- **Give options** *'Instead of fighting over the swing, let's find something you can both do. Would you like to play on the slide or in the sandpit?'* Giving them a choice can bypass the original dispute altogether.

- **Say it in a word** *'Noise!'* One word can work better than a long, boring explanation (don't worry, they know what you mean).

- **Describe what you see** *'You both want a boiled egg, but there's only one egg left.'* If you put the problem into words in a neutral voice, it can take a lot of heat out of the situation. Then your children may be able to come up with a solution.

- **Ask what comes next** *'You've knocked into her by accident. What should you do?'* You're more likely to get a genuine apology (and thus end the argument) if you don't tell your child off or force him to apologize.

- **Whisper** *'It's not kind to speak to people that way.'* It's a good way to get your point across without adding to the tension.

- **Give thanks in advance** *'Thanks for working out a way to share the art box.'* If you manage to slip this in extremely early, it can even prevent an argument breaking out. It opens up the possibility that they can negotiate instead of going straight to squabbling.

- **Refer to the rules** *'In this house, we don't push people.'* You're not ordering them to stop, just reminding them of the rules – bonus points if you set up these rules ahead of time.

Give information Another wonderful way to get your point across without diving headlong into a battle is to give information in a matter-of-fact voice. This works because you're not getting into a conflict you could lose. Your children probably won't defy you because you aren't telling them to do something (or to stop doing it). You're simply giving them the words to describe what's going on:

- *'You both want to hold the guinea pig. But it's not working and he's getting frightened.'*
- *'Jack didn't mean to hurt you. He was carrying a big bag and accidentally knocked into you as he went past.'*
- *'Now that Rosie can crawl and pull herself upright, she can reach your things if you leave them on the table.'*

Once children can see why the situation is going wrong, they're more likely to be reasonable.

Try telling your children that apologizing is often the quickest, most efficient way to resolve an argument.

❛ My children got into a big fight because my daughter drew pictures on a notebook my son was saving for a project. The accusations and insults were hideous. Neither of them could see a way out of it.

So I told my daughter her best shot at ending it would be to apologize. At first she refused, but in the end she shouted, 'Well I'M SORRY!' He was quiet for a few seconds, and then he shouted back, 'Well why didn't you just say that in the first place?' ❜

Giving information can also help when neither child will back down. If they know that it's OK to have different views, they might stop fighting.

❛ My son accused my daughter of throwing a magazine at him on purpose. She insisted she'd just tried to toss it on the table. They were at a stalemate, so I said, 'It's clear neither of you is going to change your mind. So there's no point arguing any longer. You're just going to have to agree to disagree, and leave it.' ❜

Express your feelings If you can tell your children how you feel about the fighting in a straightforward way, they may take you seriously:

- ❛I'm not enjoying this lunch. I can't relax when you keep picking on each other.'

This is more subtle and more effective than telling them they're behaving like pigs and ordering them to stop messing around. Again, you aren't giving them a chance to say no, just expressing how you feel. With a bit of luck they'll do the right thing.

Stand your ground If none of this is working, it might be time to take things up a notch. But this doesn't mean shouting orders up the stairs or making threats from the next room. Instead, **Commando Parents** make sure they're in the same room and get eye contact with their children when they want action.

Then they might firmly say what they expect and rather than repeating themselves or shouting, they stand there looking stern until their children behave. They try to give the impression they can wait all day if necessary.

> *I used to get hoarse, begging my children to stop annoying me with their silly little arguments. But now I've changed my tactics and it seems to be working. It takes a bit of nerve, but I tell them to cut it out, then wait with my arms folded. They soon get the message that I'm not going to change my mind or go away. They don't like me hovering over them, so they'll usually start being nicer to each other.*

Standing your ground can be harder with older children, but if you have some natural authority and they're not yet wound up in a complicated argument, it can work. Even if it doesn't and you have to use consequences, you haven't lost anything. If you don't give any outward sign that the argument is getting to you (shouting, pleading or walking off in a huff are usually the giveaways), you won't lose any authority.

Use consequences What do you do if you've tried everything, nothing works and you need to put an end to the argument? Try **Commando** consequences.

Consequences work much better if you give your children a bit of warning. So instead of resorting to punishments straight away, warn them. Let them know what'll happen if they don't do what you say.

So instead of:

- *'Give me that toy RIGHT NOW!'*

try:

- *'If you don't stop fighting over that toy, I'll take it away.'*

Instead of:

- *'Leave the table. This instant!'*

try:

- *'If you don't stop flicking peas, you will have to leave the table.'*

The trouble with sibling rivalry is it can be difficult to come up with an obvious consequence. You might try:

- *'If you don't stop being mean to your sister, she'll be angry and upset about it.'*

But if one child is deliberately trying to wind up another, this is probably the exact outcome he wants. So if necessary, give him the consequence of being temporarily separated from the rest of the family. Try:

- *'People don't want to be with you if you:*
  mess up their things
  annoy them
  hit them
  pull their hair
  shout like that [or whatever].
  So please go to your room for half an hour.'

Thoughts on Time Out

Instead of allowing your children to keep bugging each other for hours on end, separating them allows them a little time alone to put the problem into perspective and start afresh. When they come back, they are far more likely to be reasonable.

Lots of parents find time out really useful.

'It works well if I offer time out as a refuge. Sometimes my children need a chance to get away from each other and calm down.'

However, others are ambivalent about it.

'I couldn't give time out as a punishment when my boys were little because they refused to go. Then it just became another thing to fight about. Another drama.'

There are lots of variations on time out.
Some parents send children to their own rooms, some send them out of the room altogether, others send them to separate parts of the room they're in.

'I give them each a book and tell them they have to face different directions. At the very least they can practise their reading.'

Even if your children insist they like time out, that's absolutely fine.

'Time out gives you time to think and understand the situation. Then you know what you've done wrong, as well as what the other person has done wrong. Once you've thought of it, it doesn't seem like such a big thing.'

But some children hate it.

'Time out is a stupid waste of time. If my mum sent me to my room I'd just mess it up.'

It might help if you try explaining what happens on a physiological level. When people get angry or upset, their bodies produce lots of stress hormones. So they might need a break to let their adrenaline levels get back to normal.

Some children had advice to pass on to parents.

'It can be good, as long as Mum doesn't shout, "Right, I've had enough! You two go out and think about what you've done." It's better if she says, "Go and calm down for a bit. We'll discuss it later".'

'Time out would be better if it was only ten or fifteen minutes long. It gives you a chance to calm down and be reasonable. But if you're stuck for an hour, it just gets you furious.'

When consequences work, your children know what to expect and probably won't argue about them.

> My sister-in-law's children are really well behaved. If they're ever rude to each other, she makes them apologize straight away. If they refuse, they have to go straight to their bedroom until they are ready to say sorry.
>
> She doesn't have to yell at them and arguments never seem to get out of hand. I wish we had a lovely atmosphere like that in our house.

But lots of parents find they have trouble being a **Commando Parent** and intervening in their children's arguments. If you find you have to nag and shout, or beg and plead, to get any kind of action, what can you do.

But It's Not Working . . .

'This Commando stuff doesn't work with my children. I try to be firm, but I still have to ask them a hundred times to stop fighting.'

If you don't think you're cut out to be a **Commando Parent**, life can be stressful and frustrating. The place to start is by strengthening your authority by borrowing some **Sorted Parent** tools.

Try being a SORTED PARENT

Set up rules and give advance warning The secret of **Sorted Parents** is that they think ahead. Because they set up rules beforehand, they find they don't need to be so tough at the very moment they want their children to stop fighting. So they tell their children in advance how they expect them to behave and what the consequences will be for stepping out of line. They also give everyone plenty of warning that things are going to change, so they have time to get used to the idea:

- *'Starting next week, if anyone snatches a toy, they'll have to go straight to their room for fifteen minutes. Just to let you know, it's not worth arguing about this one. Time out will double to thirty minutes if you're stroppy about it.'*

If the new rule is a major change in your family, try giving about a week's notice, with a couple of reminders, before you actually start enforcing it. If it's a minor change, a couple of days should do.

Instead of hissing at your children on the walk to school as they head butt each other off the kerb into the road, you'll have more authority if you tell them ahead of time what behaviour you expect:

- *'When we're walking to school, I expect you NOT to push and pull each other. It's dangerous and I don't want one of you to get knocked into the road in front of a lorry. If you start shoving each other, I'll have to walk between you.'*

Bite the bullet One of the best ways to strengthen your authority is to decide what you care about and get those grey areas clear in your own mind. You might need to do some hard thinking about what is and isn't acceptable. Do you allow jokey comments at the table? Or pillow fights and horse-play at bedtime? You may all enjoy the fun, until things go too far. If sometimes you allow things and sometimes you don't, it's harder to clamp down when you can't tolerate any more mayhem. The clearer you are in your own mind, the easier it will be to tell your children what you expect.

If you think ahead and use these **Sorted** tools, there's far less chance of rebellion when you have to be a **Commando** and enforce them. So when it comes to the crunch and you tell your children to stop snatching, pushing, teasing or whatever else they're doing, they might just do what you say.

Of course, they might also test you to see if you're really serious. But the good news is that you will probably look and sound different. You'll be clear, you'll seem as if you mean business and you'll feel more confident about following through. Over time, as you notch up more successes, you'll find it all gets easier.

'My children know the rules. But sometimes they don't care. They get so angry with each other they won't listen to me. What can I do?'

If you want to break up an argument quickly, it helps to get your timing right. You'll find it's a hundred times easier if you can get in there at the beginning. If it's too late and everyone's already wound up, a short, sharp intervention simply won't work.

> ❟ My children mostly argue about such petty things that I can usually stop them straight away by telling them to cut it out.
>
> But if they won't stop, there's probably more to it. Then I know I have to listen and find out what's been happening. ❟

We'll talk you through calming down arguments (see pages 161–4).

Try being a PHYSICAL PARENT

It's also worth bearing in mind that if your children aren't feeling well – if they're exhausted, hungry or stir-crazy from being cooped up inside – it's no use being a **Commando** because they won't listen. They're almost bound to keep fighting and overreacting until they've had a nap, a decent snack or a blast of fresh air.

'You say to separate them and send them to their rooms. But my children are teenagers. Fat chance! There's no way I could get them to go.'

You can easily lift up little ones and take them out of the combat zone, but as children get bigger it gets more difficult. By the time they're teenagers, you can't wrestle them out of the room if they don't want to go. So what else can you do? Try consequences that are meaningful to them. Remind them that pocket money, computer and TV time, or lifts to friends' houses aren't basic human rights.

- 'I can't stand the noise any longer. If you two don't stop, I may not feel like doing you any favours. Next time you ask me for a lift or want to go clothes shopping, I might not be in the mood to take you.'

'Is there anything else I can do to get my children to sort things out for themselves?'

Try being a LAID-BACK PARENT

Ask for solutions It's fine to be a **Commando Parent** and let your children know, in no uncertain terms, that their fighting has got to stop. But you can also encourage them to take responsibility for their behaviour by telling them to come up with the solution themselves. They may just need a firm instruction from you to get on with it.

Try:

- 'By arguing like this over the remote control, you're both missing your programmes. I want you two to come up with a compromise now.'

- 'I don't like this shouting and your sister is crying. Find a better way to tell her how you feel.'

- 'This has gone on long enough. You've got to find a way to divide that Lego. I'll give you five minutes to come up with a good idea.'

If they look at you blankly, or the arguing gets worse, they may need more help before they can find solutions on their own. See pages 174–85 on brainstorming for more advice.

'I'm good at making my children stop. But sometimes afterwards, the argument flares up again. It drives me mad.'

If you're a natural **Commando**, you might think you've dealt with the trouble if you get your children to stop fighting immediately or send them to their rooms for time out. But if they're still feeling hard done by, you've inadvertently buried the problem rather than solved it. Either the argument will start up again, or there'll be an undercurrent of unexpressed, bottled-up resentment that can last for hours, days or even years.

I wasn't allowed to be nasty to my sister. My parents simply wouldn't have it. If they caught me, they'd come down really hard on me.

So I went underground and did things behind their back. Once they'd put us to bed, I'd order my sister around, making her fetch me tissues and glasses of water like a little personal slave.

I'd also be really mean to her and tell her she was stupid. I was horrible to her. I still feel bad about it.

So however good you are at being a **Commando**, and however good things appear to be on the surface, it's always worth double-checking what's going on underneath. Here's how to do it.

Try being a TUNED-IN PARENT

Wait for a good moment and then check how each child feels:

- *'Thanks for handing the iPod to me instead of tussling over it. Was that the end of the argument?'*
- *'I was so impressed when you went straight to your room to calm down. Are you still angry with her?'*
- *'It was kind of you to let him watch the semi-finals. Are you still disappointed you missed your programme?'*

Chewing over feelings and rehashing arguments can seem like a big waste of your time, and you may not want to dive back into a bad place. But if you take even five minutes to tune in, you can save yourself a lot of trouble in the long run. This is the time your children can offload why they were arguing, how they feel (or felt), or whether something really serious was going on.

Even if you think that one child is obviously the aggressor and the other is clearly the victim, you need to listen to both sides of the story. If you can untangle their feelings and get to the crux of their problem, you may even be able to stop the same thing happening again. If your children are reluctant to talk to you or you find it tricky to talk about feelings, see the advice below and also in Chapter 3 on jealousy and resentment.

Calm Things Down

Your fourth option in an argument is to try to calm things down. Sometimes it's your only option. If one child is already in tears and the other is making death threats, you obviously can't ignore the problem and it's too late to nip it in the bud. If they're very wound up, asking them to solve it themselves isn't going to work either. At this point your best way forward is to try to defuse the tension.

When it works, it's great for everybody: you won't need to shout (so no guilt – hooray!) and your children will feel you understand them. If you also manage to help them resolve their differences and become friends again, it's one of those wonderful moments when you'll want to raise both your hands in the air and shout 'Victory!' at the top of your voice.

But we know it's not always easy to calm everyone down in a crisis, so we'll talk you through each step. Once you find you can bring heated discussions down from boiling point to comfortable, you'll begin to feel confident about tackling even complicated arguments.

How To Do It
Try being a TUNED-IN PARENT

Tuned-In Parents are fantastic at cooling down difficult situations and untangling arguments. By listening and getting to the root of why their children are fighting, they can stop a lot of arguments from recurring. By showing their children how to listen and mediate, they can also help them learn to negotiate peace treaties on their own. Here are some of their secrets.

Listen to their feelings Tuning in and listening is a brilliant way to bring simple disputes to an end. Lots of parents find it works even better than ignoring the fighting or being firm. It can be quick, simple, bring your children closer and also make them feel closer to you.

Untangling more complicated problems isn't always easy and can take time. However sympathetic you set out to be, it can be quite a feat to listen patiently. But tuning in may be your best hope of salvaging the situation so that everyone ends up happy. The simplest way to start is by acknowledging how each child is feeling. Try:

- *'I see you're both upset,'*

or:

- *'Joe, it looks like you're furious with your brother. Mitch, you don't look happy either.'*

Then ask them to take it in turns to tell you what happened, with no interruptions. Don't take sides or tell one of them off, even if it's incredibly tempting. Just listen and confirm that you've heard them:

- *'I see. So you were annoyed with him for humming that Teletubbies song because it gets stuck in your head. And you got really angry because he wouldn't stop.'*
- *'And you're upset because he pushed you over. You feel you should be allowed to hum whenever you want.'*
- *'You think he only hums to annoy you.'*

And so on . . .

This might seem to take for ever, but if you don't listen, their feelings can smoulder away, ready to re-ignite. When they aren't discussed or given a chance to be resolved, all sorts of trivial issues can become much bigger than they need to be.

❻ *My sister and I used to fight about all sorts of stupid things. I remember one huge one about who got to wear the pink penguin pyjamas.*

But really we were fighting lots of battles. Underneath every petty squabble were the unsolved issues from before.

We never got to the bottom of it all. I'd like to think we've grown out of it, but there are some subjects that are still explosive. There are so many feelings intertwined. ,,

Even if the issues are small, they can arouse big emotions, but once you show you've heard and understood every cross or unhappy feeling, the storm should die down. It's wonderful how well listening can work. If you're lucky, your children will feel so much better that they might even skip off and forget all about their quarrel.

Accept difficult feelings Unfortunately tuning in isn't always easy. Sometimes it's more like an archaeological dig: as you go deeper, you can find mindboggling layers of accusations and counter-accusations, with both children getting angrier as they relate their side of the story. If you can, hold your nerve, keep your temper and carry on listening.

Some parents find the complexity of their children's arguments so daunting or annoying that they don't want to listen. Others find it hard to tune in because of the sheer intensity of their children's feelings. They can't bear to delve into their arguments because they feel sick or anxious as the emotion comes to the surface. Lots of parents find it literally painful to hear the things their children say. If your daughter calls her brother 'A freak! A moron!', or your son says he wishes he was an only child, 'Just send her away. Send her to an orphanage!' it's easy to panic and tell them not to say those awful things. But if you don't listen properly, you may be letting yourself in for further aggravation because your child may become even more angry or obstinate.

Think of it as a pressure cooker. The pressure dissipates more quickly if you let the steam out instead of clamping down the lid. You aren't agreeing that your son is an idiot, or that you'd all be better off if you put your daughter up for adoption. You're only accepting that they're furious about something their sibling has said or done. Once your children feel understood, their anger will begin to dissipate and they'll be much less likely to take it out on their brothers and sisters. So try:

- 'Yes. I can see you're furious.'
- 'I understand why that bothers you.'

As long as you're even handed and listen to both children, it can work miracles. Once they've let off some steam they'll begin to calm down, and then, at last, you can help them to bring the argument to some sort of resolution.

But It's Not Working . . .

'I'm so tired, and my to-do list is two pages long. I haven't got the time or the patience to listen to all their petty grievances.'

Children's trivial, pointless, unreasonable arguments can drive most of us demented. You may not want to spend hours listening to every little nuance of who did what and why. It can be tedious and seem like such a complete waste of time, especially when you're already busy. It's often tempting to cut the whole thing short, tell them to grow up and dish out punishments just to put an end to it.

But if their emotions are complicated, you need to get right to the bottom of them, or their feelings of injustice will still be there. With luck, the more you listen, the less your children will fight. Eventually, you might find that the arguments aren't as annoying and overwhelming as they used to be.

If you honestly aren't up to tuning in – you really can't face it – try pausing instead. It's better than jumping in, shouting and making a hash of things. Leave them to it until you can listen. Their argument might go on longer or become more intense, which isn't ideal, but tuning in later is better than not tuning in at all.

'But why do I have to get so involved? I want my children to learn to solve their own problems.'

It's great when siblings can sort things out for themselves, but if they don't yet know how to listen to each other, things can easily turn ugly.

> ❛ My children were fighting in the car. So I parked on the driveway and said, 'Fine. You two can just stay in here until you're ready to behave.'
>
> Well, they stayed in that car for two hours. When they came out, they both had scratches all over their faces! It was so embarrassing; people kept asking them, and me, what happened.
>
> I can't leave it all up to them. I don't want a trip to A&E, and they are heading that way. ❜

If they can't solve their own arguments, you may have to help them calm down and express themselves reasonably. It isn't easy, even for adults – that's why we have lawyers and the United Nations. So you may have to show your children many times how to listen to each other before they start getting it on their own. You'll know they're starting to make progress when you overhear them explaining their views instead of getting into a blazing row.

'I'd like to tune in, but things get so heated I can't get a word in edgeways.'

Given half a chance, most children are pretty upfront about things and will take the opportunity to tell you what happened, or at least the version of it they'd like you to hear. But if they're so embroiled in an argument that they ignore all your attempts to mediate, then try another option. You could pause or separate them until things have calmed down.

'I'm tuning in and trying to get the story straight, but they keep interrupting each other.'

Try being a COMMANDO PARENT

Give information Try explaining that they need to take turns:

- 'You want a chance to tell what happened and it's only fair your brother gets a chance too. So you need to stop interrupting each other.'

Be very clear, even obvious about it, because when they're having a go at each other they might not be thinking straight:

- 'First one of you tells your side of the story while the other person stays quiet. Then the other one gets to talk without being interrupted. You'll each have plenty of chances to speak.'

When the next storm blows up, they may remember what you said, or you can remind them:

- 'Do you remember the rules? While the other person is speaking, you need to listen. Then it will be your turn.'

If they still won't respect each other's time to speak, you may have to call a halt to things until later. Then, in a quiet moment, long before the next argument, you can try again.

'At least yours talk. Half the time mine won't say anything at all.'

If you've got a child who is reluctant to talk, try tuning in to that feeling directly:

- 'It looks as though you don't want to discuss this.'

If this doesn't work and he just sits there glowering and seething, you could always try later.

Lots of children don't like to open up and talk about their feelings when they're upset. They may feel invaded or vulnerable. As children have told us:

❛ I really don't like talking when I'm angry. When I start to explain how I feel, I get a lump in my throat and feel like I'm about to cry. So I don't want to. ❜

❛ I don't want to tell my brothers and sisters how I feel. They'll say, 'Who cares? You're a loser.' ❜

Others don't like talking because they don't think they should have to explain how they feel; everyone should just know. But it's difficult for parents if you're expected to be a mind-reader.

Whatever the reason, there's no need to force information out of your child. The conversation will be a thousand times more productive if you wait and bring up the subject again when he's less emotional. He might appreciate it if you guess how he's feeling so he doesn't have to make the first move himself. Start with neutral statements rather than questions:

- *'You must have been furious after being called a zit-face. That might explain why you snatched her book.'*

Don't worry that you'll get it wrong. You'll probably be more accurate than you think, and even if you're not, he'll set you straight:

- *'No. I snatched the book because it's mine, I'm in the middle of it and she stole it without asking me.'*

'My children talk all right, but they never give me the whole story.'

When you're trying to get to the bottom of a sibling argument, lots of children only give you half-truths. It's a rare child who will readily admit exactly what he's done.

> *My son came running to me when his older sister hit him, but somehow 'forgot' to mention that he drove her absolutely demented by stealing her pencil case and refusing to give it back. It would be so much easier if he'd just admit his part in it from the beginning.*

Lots of children are economical with the truth because they're subtly trying to make themselves look as clean and innocent as possible. As one child said:

> *If I tell my mum anything about our fights, I make my faults look tinier and make my sister's look enormous.*

If you didn't see exactly what happened, or what went on beforehand, your best option is to keep tuning in to both sides so you can tease out the details. If your children are generally honest, you'll usually find that the truth lies somewhere in the middle.

It's more difficult if you suspect one of your children is deliberately trying to mislead you. If you find out that he's been blatantly lying, you might have to wonder why he's doing it.

If he makes things up to keep himself out of trouble, it may be worth thinking about how you handle your children's arguments. If you tend to come down hard and punish them, you could be part of the problem. As we've mentioned in Chapter 3 pages 87–8, your children might not feel the need to lie if you listen with an open mind and see their mistakes as things that can be put right.

'When my children get angry, they push me to take sides. What do I do?'

If your child is convinced he's right and tries to manipulate you into punishing the others, it can be hideously stressful.

> Most sibling arguments in our house are about perceived injustices, and my children get very worked up about them. They've all got a highly developed sense of right and wrong, particularly when it comes to themselves.
>
> They each think they're one hundred per cent right, and they want instant retribution. 'Send her to her room', 'Take away his pocket money', 'Smack him'. And I've never smacked anyone! They're so hell-bent on reprisals, it's exhausting.

Try being a TUNED-IN PARENT

Listen to their feelings Before you pass any judgements, you need to find out what really happened by listening to both sides of the story. There may be more to it than you realize. Listening may be enough to calm both sides down, but if it isn't . . .

Try being a PAUSE PARENT

Wait until later Don't allow your children to bully you into taking sides or dishing out punishments. If necessary, tell them you need time to think about it. You don't have to solve every problem straight away, and if everyone is stressed it's probably better to wait.

When you've given yourself time to think things through, you will be more rational and so will they. Then if you tune in to your children's feelings you might find you can solve the whole thing.

'When I listen to my children, I often find they're both right. What do I do then?'

Try being a LAID-BACK PARENT

Be a role model Once you tune in, you can often see a way to solve a sibling argument, but if you find that both your children have a good point, one way forward is to be a good role model. If you're honest and show that you're capable of being sympathetic, apologetic or open-minded, it can make it easier for your children to be the same.

Here's how one mother got herself out of a difficult situation.

One day, as I was scraping plates into the bin, I noticed my grandmother's ring had dropped off my finger. I foraged through the rubbish like some crazy old street lady, but couldn't find it.

When I collected my son from nursery, he told me he'd help, and I said I'd give him a pound if he found it. We spent the next two hours hunting all over the kitchen and living room, but no luck.

When we collected my daughter from school, she also volunteered to help. I said I'd give them each fifty pence for looking, and a pound to the person who found it.

My daughter put on rubber gloves, plunged her hands back into the bin and found the ring in two minutes flat.

Her brother burst into tears. 'I hate you. You shouldn't get the pound. It was my idea to look for the ring, and you were in my way so I couldn't look properly.'

'Don't worry,' I said, 'I'll give you both a pound; I'm so happy to have it back.'

Then my daughter burst into tears. 'That's not fair! You're only being nice to him because he's younger. You always favour him. You wouldn't give me a pound if he'd found it.'

What could I do? Suddenly I had two furious children. I was tempted to yell that neither of them would get any money if they carried on like that, but I managed to restrain myself.

I turned to my daughter. 'I don't really know what to do. I'm so happy you've found my ring so quickly. But in some ways I wish I hadn't asked you because Arthur was already helping me.'

Then I turned to my son and said, 'I am so glad I've got my ring back. And I'm so grateful for all your help. But I know you're disappointed you didn't find it.'

Then I said to both of them, 'And I'm also so sorry I even mentioned money, because you both feel you deserve it. Now you're both crying and I don't know what to do about it.'

What happened next was amazing. Arthur said, 'I think Rachel deserves the money – she did find it.'

Rachel said, 'I'm going to buy sweets with the money and I'll share them with Arthur.'

It was a miracle! 🎤

Some parents don't like showing any weakness. But if you're big enough to admit that you get it wrong sometimes and don't know all the answers, it gives your children the freedom to be generous in return. If you suspect that your children often argue because they don't want to back down or lose face, this will help them see that if everyone gives way a little, it's easier to meet somewhere in the middle.

You've got four different options when you need to stop a fight. You could try being a:

- **Laid-Back Parent** Ask your children for ideas. You might be surprised how quickly and easily they can solve their own problems.

- **Pause Parent** Stay out of the low-level bickering, keep calm and don't give your children attention for fighting.

- **Commando Parent** Be firm and act quickly. This can prevent a lot of aggravation.

- **Tuned-In Parent** Listen to feelings, so you can untangle even complicated situations.

But they all lead back to the same place. You're aiming to reach some sort of equilibrium, where the atmosphere's good and everyone's speaking to each other again.

Being able to stop an argument, whether by doing less or by doing more, is quite an achievement. But you can go even further. Next we'll show you ways to encourage your children to get on better so they don't feel so much like arguing.

5

Strengthening Your Children's Relationship

So They Get On Better

Wouldn't it be nice to get to the point where your children enjoyed each other's company, didn't have much to fight about, and if there was a problem they could sort it out quite easily between them? Here are all sorts of ways you can help to strengthen your children's relationship:

- **Teach them to problem-solve**
  If your children get into the habit of solving their own problems, they are less likely to fight now and in the future. You can show them how to do it, either by brainstorming as a family or talking to them individually.

- **Put an end to irritating behaviour and bullying**
  If your children annoy each other, small niggling issues can easily become major problems and even lead to bullying. But you can help resolve their feelings and show them what to do instead.

- **Show them how to say sorry**
  A genuine apology can draw a line under an argument and make everyone feel better. If your children are reluctant, we'll show you how to get them into better habits.

- **Encourage them to be kind to each other**
  If you praise your children when they're getting along, they're more likely to carry on.

- **Help them to build shared experiences**
  When siblings have fun together, they'll store up good memories for the rest of their lives.

Teach Them to Problem-Solve

If your children tend to argue over recurring problems, you need to help them come up with long-term solutions. You might be familiar with the kind of situations we mean. Do your children argue over and over about what to watch on TV, whose turn it is to use the computer, where they sit in the car, who's not helping to clean up, who got a longer bedtime story, or because they want the same toy? You might be able to resolve a specific incident (see Chapter 4) but at some point they'll just start fighting over the same issue again.

Don't worry: you won't have to put up with their squabbling for ever. You can help your children solve their problems, either as a family or by talking to each child individually, and we'll show you how.

Brainstorm and Ask Your Children for Solutions

One of the best ways to help your children solve recurring problems is to sit down together and ask them for ideas. But it doesn't have to be that formal. You might already be brainstorming without realizing it, simply by discussing things while you're all sitting round the kitchen table or walking to school.

At its simplest, it's about being a **Laid-Back Parent** – asking your children for suggestions and then deciding on a solution. There's every chance they'll feel flattered to be consulted, the more problems you can solve together, the happier everyone will be. You can avoid a huge amount of daily stress when they stop battling over the same old things.

By encouraging your children to discuss things openly all

together, you're teaching them useful life skills which will serve them well into adulthood, including:

- *Expressing their views calmly and clearly*
- *Listening to other people without interrupting*
- *Behaving well, even when they disagree (no eye-rolling or patronizing noises)*
- *Negotiating without shouting*
- *Compromizing*

It's also far better to air grievances and feelings in a supportive environment than to allow fixed behaviour patterns to remain unacknowledged and unchallenged.

When we get together, our oldest brother always treats us the way he did when we were children. He's bossy, boastful and plays little mind games to put the rest of us down. We've never progressed beyond this and we can't be bothered to challenge him now. If we'd dealt with it when we were kids, our relationship with him would be a lot straighter.

Brainstorming can be a great way to solve all kinds of issues. But even if your family discussions tend to be volatile, we will give you lots of ideas to make brainstorming work for you.

Before the meeting
Try being a PAUSE PARENT

Wait until later Don't rush straight in. Timing is everything and there's no point starting a discussion with your children when you are stressed, furious or emotional. Wait until you can sound friendly and string a rational sentence together, preferably at the same time. If necessary, go for a walk or, if you're really irritated, get a good night's sleep first.

It's also not worth sitting your children down for a discussion if they are already wound up. So, for example, don't bother if they're already bickering about whose turn it is to clear the plates. Instead, try talking to them long before the next meal.

Try being a SORTED PARENT

Bite the bullet You may have tried to solve recurring problems before and become discouraged. If you're feeling overwhelmed, you may not think you have the energy or courage to face them again. But if your children can't work things out amongst themselves, it's up to you to keep trying to help them.

One good way to start is by just thinking. Block out some time to work out where to start, either with an easy problem or one that drives you absolutely mad. You might also think through the best way to bring up the topic. With a little bit of thought, it'll be easier than you expect.

During the meeting
Try being a LAID-BACK PARENT

Ask the family for ideas Start by getting everyone to sit together. Explain the problem, then give them a chance to speak one at a time. Try:

- *'I don't like the way you've been treating each other and it's been going on for long enough. How could you get along better?'*
- *'How can we make sure this doesn't keep happening?'*

or:

- *'What do you think would be fair for everyone?'*

Try being a CHEERLEADER PARENT

Praise on the spot You might be impressed by the ingenuity of their solutions. Even if you're not, try giving your children lots of encouragement and feedback to keep the ideas and conversation flowing. You might try:

- *'That's a good idea. I'll write it down.'*

- *'Interesting way round it. Thank you for that.'*

Writing down all their suggestions, no matter how silly or impractical, can make children feel that the meeting is important and their ideas are important too. If you keep giving them the message that they're good at working things out, it will encourage them to carry on.

Try being a TUNED-IN PARENT

Listen to their feelings If this is a regular problem or an explosive one, your children may have strong views about it and each other. Keep listening and acknowledging what they say so that they know you understand. It's your best way of taking everyone's views into account and keeping the meeting on track.

Some of their claims and counter-claims might seem like a big waste of time, especially if you think one child is being unreasonable. But if they can let off steam and feel they've been heard, there's more chance that they'll come to an agreement in the end.

Try being a COMMANDO PARENT

Give orders that don't sound like orders You can, and should, be in charge of running the brainstorming session so your children don't start rowing again. Encourage them to take turns, so they know that they'll get a fair chance to speak. If they're getting frustrated, you might also need to reassure them:

- *'Don't worry. You have to wait your turn, but you'll each get as many turns as you need.'*

It's also important to make it clear that they can't interrupt or put down other people's ideas, no matter how ridiculous they sound:

- *'Even though you don't like Rachel's idea, let's listen to everyone's suggestions before we decide which one to choose.'*

Express your feelings There's nothing that says you can't make suggestions too. If you remain democratic and resist the urge to get heavy or preachy with your ideas, your children are more likely to be open to what you have to say. Of course, you can also retain veto power so you don't have to agree to any solution you aren't happy with.

Try being a LAID-BACK PARENT

Ask for solutions Once you've all come up with a list of suggestions, it might be obvious to you which one is best. But keep being a **Laid-Back Parent** and ask your children once again what they think. The more involved they feel in coming up with a good solution to the problem, the more incentive they'll have to make it work.

As you help your children whittle down the ideas on the list, you can all discuss them again. Even if the discussion gets heated, they might just surprise you and come to the same conclusion you did.

You should get your children to agree on the repercussions if (when!) they ignore the new plan and the same old thing happens again. Also try to make sure that the consequences are enforceable, because it's going to be up to you to do it.

Try being a SORTED PARENT

Set up rules Once you've all reached an agreement, write down the details so there are no grey areas. When is it going to start? How long are you going to try it? What will the consequences be if anyone breaks the rule? To make things even clearer, you might try posting the agreement up on the wall where everyone can see it.

You can also suggest a follow-up meeting in a couple of days or weeks to discuss how it's going. This might sound too organized to be true, but it can be a good move. If your children don't feel that they're going to be locked into the new agreement for ever, they may be more willing to give it a proper chance. If it works out well, you might not need to discuss it at all, and if it doesn't, it's no bad thing to make some adjustments.

After the meeting
Try being a SORTED PARENT

Train them up If it's a big change, it might be better to start in a few days so that everyone has a chance to get used to the idea. Remind your children a couple of times what's going to happen and when, so they're mentally prepared for it and there's less chance they'll forget or rebel when the time comes.

- *'So starting on Monday you'll take turns to tidy up the kitchen, and there'll be a list on the fridge of who's doing what.'*

Try being a TUNED-IN PARENT

Listen to their feelings Don't worry if their enthusiasm is short-lived and they grumble about the new plan. If they complain, then listen, but don't change your mind. This is your big chance to sort this problem once and for all. So stand firm, keep listening and eventually your children should stop moaning.

Try being a CHEERLEADER PARENT

Praise on the spot If you notice when your children are doing things right and thank them or compliment them for it, they've got more incentive to carry on. Even if you're the type who tends to switch off and forget to mention when your children are behaving well, do something to make sure you remember. Stick a post-it note on the bathroom mirror, steering wheel, fridge or wherever to remind yourself to say something nice.

Notice the good, ignore the bad Also, try to find something positive to say about the times that don't go quite so well so they don't seem like such a failure. If you or your children are feeling discouraged, it's easy to give up. But if you can keep everyone's morale up, including your own, temporary blips won't be a problem. It might seem strange at first, but if you think hard enough, there's almost always something positive you can say.

- *'Thanks for apologizing when you forgot it was your turn to feed the dog. Your sister really appreciated it.'*

Once you feel you're making some progress with one problem, you can start again and focus on another one.

'I love the thought of my children brainstorming, but they just look blank and don't say anything. What am I doing wrong?'

Try being a LAID-BACK PARENT

If your children haven't done any kind of problem-solving before, they might find the whole process a bit strange or even embarrassing. But like anything new, it will get easier the more they do it. You could start them off with less contentious issues:

- *'I'm going to the supermarket. What shall we have for dinner?'*
- *'Here's the TV guide. Have a look and then let's choose two or three programmes you'd like to record this week.'*

The idea is to make it worth speaking up because there is no right or wrong answer. No one's opinions are more important than anyone else's and the adults in the house will take you seriously. Then follow up by cooking something that they've chosen or letting them watch the programmes they like.

When you start brainstorming, some children jump right in and start talking. But others may stay quiet because they're worried that their ideas aren't good enough. Just keep encouraging them to have a go:

- *'I'd really like to hear your views. It doesn't matter how wild they are. Throw out some suggestions, I'll write them all down, and then we can talk about them.'*

You may also find it helps to keep reminding your children that they aren't allowed to put each other's ideas down.

Even if the ideas aren't flowing, you can still give them some credit for just sitting there looking at each other:

- *'This is a tough problem and I like the way you're trying to think your way round it.'*

It's subtle, but if you compliment your children for thinking, they may just start doing it.

'I can't believe it. We did the whole brainstorming thing and I thought we'd solved the problem. But now they're at it again!'

Try being a COMMANDO PARENT

Don't despair. If your children start up again, you have a lot more authority than you did before. If you're lucky, you may only need to give them a quick reminder – 'You know what we agreed' – and they'll stop arguing.

If this doesn't work, remind them of the consequences and be tough if you have to. Stop the car, confiscate the Gameboys or do whatever it was you all decided you'd do if it happened again. You aren't being mean; your children already know the deal and if you show them you mean business, they're more likely to start being reasonable again.

Try being a PAUSE PARENT

If your children have been squabbling over something for ages, it's unrealistic to expect them to change overnight and stop fighting for ever. Over time they may forget the rules and slip back into their old habits.

Some parents lose heart at this point. When your children agree to a ceasefire, family life can be so wonderful for a while that it's doubly disappointing when they start picking on each other again. But if you expect some setbacks, it's easier not to overreact when they happen.

Think of it as a work in progress. You will almost certainly need to go back and discuss issues again to see whether the original solution is working or to make adjustments as circumstances change:

- *'You seem to be having fewer fights about the computer, except on the days when you both need it for your homework. What can we do about it?'*

Your children will appreciate you for listening to them and trying to find a way forward that suits everyone. In the long term, if you keep helping them to come up with solutions, they'll find less to fight about.

'I don't see the point of all this. Can't I just tell them to behave?'

Try being a COMMANDO PARENT

Use consequences If you're very sure of your ground or your children are quite cooperative, of course you don't need to set up a family meeting every time there's a problem. Just telling them firmly to behave is quick, simple and can nix a whole layer of arguing:

- *'I won't drive when you two are shouting about whose turn it is to choose the music. Sort it out now, or I'm turning the CD player off. If you carry on arguing, I'll be stopping the car.'*

When it works, it's marvellous. If they know you mean business, they might stop immediately. But as you probably know from experience, it's not always that easy. Lots of parents try to lay down the law and fail miserably because their children refuse to listen and carry on fighting, or they cooperate on the surface but carry on doing unpleasant things to their siblings behind their parents' backs.

Very few parents find they can solve complicated, long-running issues simply by giving orders. Instead, try sitting down with your children for a proper discussion and listening to their ideas. Then you may find they start doing the right thing whether you're there or not.

'My daughter sabotages every discussion. She hums, puts her fingers in her ears, distracts the others and makes stupid comments. It's SO irritating!'

One or more of your children may be particularly resistant. She may just love annoying you and her siblings to get a reaction. Or she may not like talking about problems because she feels guilty, doesn't want to admit her part in them or worries she's going to be told off.

Some children (like adults) simply don't like baring their feelings in public and will do anything to avoid it. Others don't want to discuss setting up new rules because the old regime actually suits them, particularly if they get away with a lot more than their siblings. Even if they're being told off, the status quo may be comfortable and they don't realize how much more pleasant life could be.

Whatever the reason, it's worth persevering with a child like this, partly because her behaviour isn't fair on the others and partly because negotiating in a reasonable way is a useful skill. If she won't behave at the family meeting, leave it for now and try talking to her later on her own (see below). Anything else you can do to connect with her (see Chapter 3) will also help.

'I think the reason my child doesn't want to participate is because she actually enjoys fighting.'

It's true! Some children refuse to cooperate or find a solution because they don't want to stop fighting. They might crave attention from their siblings or enjoy having power over them, or want your attention and know that being mean to them is a good way to get it. If they can't stand being bored, fighting may be their idea of having a good time.

If your child is getting something out of it, it can be a very hard habit to break. But for the sake of your other children, you've got to find something that works. Again, try talking to her on her own, but if this doesn't work see pages 185–91 on tackling irritating behaviour.

Talk to Your Children Separately

'That's all fine in theory, but these family brainstorming sessions are hell. It's like stirring a stick in a nest of hornets.'

If your children are perpetual fighters and there's anarchy every time you try to discuss anything, you might not achieve much in family meetings. If you find they are chaotic and stressful, with children shouting to be heard or being deliberately nasty to each other, you may be feeling despondent.

There might also be other reasons why brainstorming doesn't work for you. If your children are older and busy with lots of after-school clubs and homework, it can be hard to find a good time to get them all together to talk. If the issue is an emotional one, one child is being particularly uncooperative, or big group discussions are not your style, you may not even want to try.

But even if family meetings don't suit you, there are other things you can do. Often the easiest way is to go behind the scenes and talk to each child individually. It'll help them to calm down and they'll still get the chance to say how they feel and come up with ideas. Some parents find that bedtime works well, when their children are feeling relaxed, but choose any time that works for you. Try:

- *'We didn't get very far sorting out your problem with your sister today. Have you got any ideas?'*

Eventually, when your child realizes she's going to be taken seriously, she might be more forthcoming and cooperative. If you have a chat with each one of your children and gather their suggestions, you might be pleased to find how easy it is to get everyone's agreement.

Bit by bit, as you help them solve their trouble spots, your children will have less to fight about and, eventually, group discussions might not seem so daunting.

'Whether I brainstorm with everyone or talk to them individually, it all sounds like a lot of work. Do I really have to go through this rigmarole every time?'
No, of course you don't. But by asking your family for solutions, you're ultimately helping your children solve their own problems. There are lots of skills they need to learn along the way, including: stating their own ideas rationally, listening to other people, negotiating and compromising. The early days may be the most time-consuming, but once they get used to it and some of their most pressing problems have been solved, it will get much quicker and easier.

Put an End to Irritating Behaviour and Bullying

Siblings can annoy each other more than anyone else in the world. They can pester and needle, tease and name-call, and be rude and nasty in ways they wouldn't dream of being with anyone else. They might start messing around because they enjoy it, but even mildly obnoxious behaviour can end in tears and tit-for-tat revenge can become chronic. In extreme cases it can turn into bullying and you need to intervene because the resentment and unhappiness can last for years.

So how can you teach them to treat each other better? Brainstorming may be part of the answer, but if the problem is contentious or there's a lot of ill-will between them, your children may not want to discuss it. So often it is up to us to help them resolve their feelings, tell them how we expect them to behave and give them strategies for when their sibling is driving them mad.

We'll start with the milder end of the spectrum, when siblings bother each other, and move on to what to do when there's bullying.

When Siblings Irritate Each Other

When siblings are in the habit of aggravating each other, it can drive you crazy too. You might be desperate for them to stop, but if you jump to conclusions about who's done what, you can inadvertently make things worse. Often the dynamic is very subtle and the roles of aggressor and victim are intertwined. Just because one child is angry and defiant and the other is crying, it doesn't mean your angry child is wholly responsible and the other is an innocent victim. Aggressors can be so exasperated by victims that they become aggressive; victims are often incredibly good at being infuriating, but so discreetly that it slips under your radar.

If you're trying to remain open-minded about what happened, how can you get them to stop irritating each other? The good news is that the answer is the same regardless of whether you're speaking to the victim or the perpetrator, or whether you suspect they're both to blame.

Try being a TUNED-IN PARENT

Accept difficult feelings Start by listening to your children. It gives you a chance to find out, from your children's perspective, what went wrong. Once you understand, you're in a much better position to help them solve it long term; and once they feel understood, they're more likely to listen to your advice.

It's human nature to listen first to the child who looks more distressed, but don't assume that what she says is the whole story. She's only giving one version of it, and it's not impossible that she's twisting the facts or leaving details out to frame her sibling and put herself in a good light. So while you're tuning in to one child, don't pass judgement or criticize another. Just listen.

It's also worth remembering how common it is for both children to feel they're the victim. The obvious victim might be the one who's been yelled at or hit. But the perpetrator may have felt pushed into it and that her response was justified because her sibling was so exasperating. So tune in and listen to both sides of the story. This will also help them to calm down.

Even if they seem evenly matched and not that bothered, it can still be worth tuning in because you might find that one child is more upset than she looks.

Try being a COMMANDO PARENT

Give information The next step is to tell them what behaviour you expect and why. Sometimes you just have to state the obvious about how they're meant to treat each other. If you say it in a reasonable way, they'll be more likely to listen. Here are some things you can try:

Explain how their behaviour can affect other people

- *'You might have started by joking around, but teasing can go too far. If the other person starts looking upset, you've got to stop.'*

- 'There's no reason to say unkind things to your sister. If what you're saying is true, then why hurt her feelings? And if it's not true, then why say it at all?'

- 'Picking on people can really bother them. You might not realize, but over time it can also shake their self-confidence.'

Tell them they aren't allowed to lash out, whatever the circumstances

- 'I can see you were really angry. But being angry doesn't make it right to shout like that.'

- 'She may have upset you yesterday, but that doesn't mean you can elbow her as you walk past.'

- 'I know you're bored, but that's no excuse for kicking him.'

Tell them they have to take responsibility for their part of the problem

- 'You don't deserve to be hit or shouted at. But if she asks you over and over to stop annoying her and you keep doing it, it's no surprise if she gets wound up.'

- 'If she hit you, I'm sorry. But you hit her back, so you also did something wrong. You need to find another way to react.'

Express your feelings If your children have got into the habit of bothering each other, one very good way to make them stop and think about it is to explain to them exactly how it makes you feel.

❛ *My children used to provoke each other constantly and wouldn't stop however much I shouted or pleaded. I found it so awful that finally I said to them, 'I really can't stand hearing the things you say to each other. They're so unkind.'*

I don't think they ever knew how much it upset me, because since then they've got much better. ❜

Try being a LAID-BACK PARENT

At this point you may be in a good position to ask your children how they can make sure the same situation doesn't happen again. This may be all it takes. But if they need a bit more guidance . . .

Try being a SORTED PARENT

Train them up Instead of telling your children what they should have done, which can inflame things further, give them suggestions about what they can do *next* time their siblings are being irritating. If necessary, practise with them so that they know what to do or say. You could help them to:

Be assertive, not aggressive
If one child tends to growl at the other:

- *'Bog off or I'll kill you, you fat loser,'*

suggest:

- *'Next time he bothers you, try telling him in a straightforward way. You could say, "I don't like it when you keep bothering me and I'm trying to do my homework. Could you please leave my room?"*

or recommend she puts a note on her door:

- *'Doing homework. DON'T COME IN!'*

Let off steam
If your children tend to get nasty and hit their siblings when they're frustrated, suggest alternatives:

- *'You could go into another room, punch a pillow or run round the garden.'*

Recognize the warning signals

Whether your child aggravates her siblings unintentionally or on purpose, suggest ways she can keep herself out of trouble. Try:

- *'When you hear in your brother's voice that he's getting angry, that's the signal to leave him alone.'*

- *'You know it bothers your sister when you keep humming, so if she asks you to stop, then stop. Or go and hum in the other room where she can't hear you.'*

Find something else to do

There are thousands of things your children can do instead of pestering each other, so make some suggestions. Try:

- *'If your brother doesn't want you to bother him, you need to stop and find something else to do. You could play with the dog or you could always come and talk to me.'*

Help them to understand each other
Try being a COMMANDO PARENT

Give information Sometimes siblings act unkindly because they're upset and worried about something completely different. If their brothers and sisters don't know what's going on, they can take it personally, and before you know it the situation has escalated.

One of the most valuable things you can do is to help your children understand each other. Realizing that their sibling's mood has nothing to do with them can be very liberating for lots of children (and parents). So tell them what's going on:

- *'I know he kicked your schoolbag. I'm so sorry and I will definitely talk to him about it later. But I know that he had a horrible day at school and, for the moment, he needs us to try to be understanding.'*

- *'I heard how he snapped at you for no reason. Something else must be wrong. I'll find out what it is.'*

Once children realize they aren't necessarily the cause of their sibling's irritation, they're often surprisingly compassionate and sympathetic.

When Siblings Bully Each Other

Sometimes one sibling can bully another and make her life a misery. If the intimidation is intentional and it's really getting to your other child, you can't ignore it and you need to make it stop.

Dealing with bullying isn't easy. You may have tried many times to put an end to it. You know you've got to protect your other child, but bullies can wield power over the entire family, including you. You might be afraid of her reaction and think nothing you do or say makes a difference. Here are some strategies that will help.

Talk to the child who's being bullied
Try being a TUNED-IN PARENT

Listen and accept difficult feelings The first thing to do when one child is getting the brunt of bad treatment is to tune in and listen to her feelings. She'll be far less stressed if she knows you understand and care, and doesn't feel she has to carry the burden by herself.

But when she's very upset it can be hard for her to explain what's going on. You may be desperate to help her feel better immediately by giving her advice and telling her you'll sort it out. Most often it's no surprise who's been causing the trouble, and you might feel you want to punish the perpetrator immediately. But for the time being, just concentrate on the child who's suffering and listen. She needs to offload her feelings and you need to hear what's been happening.

So instead of:

- *'You poor sweet thing. Leave everything to me. I'll sort it out,'*

or:

- *'How dare he treat you that way! I'm going to ground him for a month!'*

stay neutral, and encourage her to talk. Try:

- *'Mmm. I see,'*

or:

- *'Yes. No wonder that hurt your feelings.'*

Don't start criticizing the accused sibling. Dealing with your other child is a separate issue, and it's better to talk to him later on his own. Until you've heard the other side, you don't have a complete picture of what's happened anyway.

Give your bullied child some strategies

Many of the strategies for dealing with irritating behaviour will also help your bullied child (see pages 186–91), but here are some more ways you can help her stay out of trouble.

Practise what she could say
Try being a SORTED PARENT

Train them up Explain to your child that her siblings probably pick on her to get a reaction. If she usually whines or gets aggressive, they'll know they've got to her, so show her what else she could do. Try:

- *'Next time your brother pesters you or calls you names, don't give him the satisfaction of showing you're upset. Just say, "That's interesting." Then carry on with what you're doing.'*

If your child is confident enough to pull it off, you can also help her come up with answers that are more assertive or humorous.

❢My son is amazing at deflecting all kinds of grief from his sisters. If one of them calls him names, he'll smile and agree. 'Yup, I'm a big fat fart. And you're a triple big fat fart!' The thing is, he does it in such a nonchalant way – without any anger at all and a bit of a cheeky smile – that nobody gets cross with him.❢

Suggest she could walk away
Try being a COMMANDO PARENT

Give information Another useful strategy is just to walk away. It's no fun for a bully to try to provoke a reaction if the other person won't engage. So try telling your child:

- *'If your brother starts being nasty, stand up straight away and walk into the next room. He'll soon realize that there's no point in carrying on. If he follows you, just come straight to me.'*

- *'If you want, tell him you'll come back and play when he's nice to you.'*

Your child might feel it's unfair if she's always the one who has to leave the room when her brother is in a bad mood. She may have a good point here, so tell her that this is only a temporary strategy: walking out of the room can give her tormentor time to calm down. But if it keeps happening, she can tell you and you'll talk to her sibling about it.

Explain it's better to tell someone
Try being a TUNED-IN PARENT

Listen to their feelings Reinforce that your child should always come and talk to you if she has a problem – even if, and especially if, her sibling has been threatening to torture her if she does. Explain that lots of bullies get away with doing terrible things to other people by intimidating them, but if everyone knows what's going on, they can be stopped.

When You Find It Hard to Lay Down the Law

Writing this book, we were told some heartbreaking stories by adults who said they'd been bullied by their siblings. They felt real injustices had occurred and their parents didn't do enough to stop it. Many children certainly feel the same way.

I tried telling my mother how horrible my brother is. But she said I was talking rubbish and I should stop making such a big fuss over nothing.

Some parents find it difficult to come down hard on the perpetrator, or even to accept that there's any bullying going on. Even if one child is complaining, they might mistakenly think she's strong enough to take care of herself, or they may not realize how much she's suffering.

They may also be sympathetic to the bully because they can see the unhappiness or frustration behind her behaviour. She may be mildly autistic, have ADHD, or have been very unwell as a baby. Or it could just be that she's having a hard time at school. They might even feel sorry for her at one level if they know how irritating the victim can be.

Often these parents can't see, or refuse to see, what's really happening or can't bear to hear one child being criticized.

My sister bullied us all. But my father didn't stop her because she was his favourite. In his eyes she couldn't do anything wrong. After a while we knew there was no point in complaining, because nothing was going to change.

Situations like this are more common in families than you might think. So you really need to pay attention and be very clear about what's actually happening. If there's any bullying going on, you need to put a stop to it, because it's not fair on your children if you don't. See pages 198–200 for effective strategies on dealing with bullies. You may also want to re-read Chapter 3 on jealousy and resentment.

Encourage her to see her part in it

Try being a LAID-BACK PARENT

Ask for solutions No child deserves to be hit or hurt by a sibling, but bullying problems aren't always clear-cut. Your child who feels put upon may not want to hear this, but remind her that if she provokes her sibling, she's also part of the problem:

- *'Your brother keeps shouting at you and manhandling you, but you keep going into his room. How could you remember to stay out and leave him in peace?'*

Your children may also come up with the solution themselves.

> My daughter used to complain all the time that her older sisters were mean to her. One weekend she went to stay with a friend who gets on much better with hers. She came home full of new insights. 'A lot of it is my fault,' she said. 'Kristen doesn't annoy her sisters like I do.'
> Since then, they've got on much better. She's stopped all the whingeing which used to make her sisters so furious and they're being much nicer to her.

Talk to the bully

If one child is clearly the aggressor, it's equally important to talk to her about it, so you can put a stop to her behaviour. Here are some strategies that will help.

Try being a PAUSE PARENT

Keep things in perspective When you think of what she's been doing to her sibling, you may think she's a disaster – a no-hoper with a mean streak. But try to keep it in perspective. We all have a good side and a bad side, and it's likely that all your children are capable of horrifying you with their behaviour. The good news is that the behaviour is taking place within your home, which gives you a chance to do something about it.

Zip your lip When your child does something heinous, you may be consumed with anger or desperate to get to the bottom of the problem. But pressurizing her into talking is likely to backfire.

> *My older son had been bullying his little brother. He said he was a disgusting little worm and threatened to beat him up unless he stayed in his bedroom every afternoon until dinner. I work all day and had a babysitter, but she was completely clueless and had no idea what was going on.*
>
> *When my younger son told me what was happening, I was furious and confronted my older son about it. He completely denied it and said he didn't know what I was talking about. He still refuses to admit anything, so what am I supposed to do?*

If your child knows what she's done wrong, she probably won't want to discuss it with you. It's no surprise, because she knows she's going to be in trouble, but it's exasperating. If she's already lied, it's very unlikely she'll admit what she's done if you threaten her.

If you suspect she's going to clam up, wait until you're both calm before you even bring up the subject. If you've already tried, try again later, but come at it from a different angle.

Try being a TUNED-IN PARENT

Accept difficult feelings Your child clearly has some strong feelings or she wouldn't have been so horrible to her sibling. Rather than finding out what's going on so you can punish her, try finding out what's going on so you can understand her. She must have had her reasons.

So instead of:

- *'What the hell have you been doing to your sister? Do you have any idea how upset you've made her? Tell me right now what's going on, or else!'*

try:

- *'I heard you had a problem with Lucy. Sounds like you've been pretty angry with her. What's up?'*

Coming at it this way can make all the difference. Once she's had a chance to explain how she feels, you can ask her how the other child might feel – but it doesn't work the other way round.

It's tough for anyone to admit their mistakes. But if you open the door for a reasonable discussion, there's every chance you might have one. We know how difficult this can be, particularly when your child's behaviour has been anything but reasonable. But children have a much better excuse for bad behaviour than we do – they're children – and you never know what the extenuating circumstances might be. It isn't uncommon, for example, for a child to bully or pick on her siblings because she's jealous of their relationship with you. If you think this might be the case, and for lots more advice on tuning in to your badly behaved child, turn to Chapter 3.

Try being a COMMANDO PARENT

If you are lucky, your child will eventually open up and talk to you about what happened and how she feels. But even if she doesn't, you're on to her and the bullying has got to stop. Here's how to make sure it doesn't happen again.

Give information Once you've heard her side, you need to give her the information she needs. You might tell her the rules:

- *'You may hate her more than anyone on the planet, but you can't squash her face in the sandbox when you're angry with her.'*

Even if she says she doesn't care, you might tell her how she makes her sibling feel:

- *'It's awful for anyone to get sand in their eyes and mouth, and it really upsets her.'*

Use consequences If you can get through and appeal to her better nature, the bullying may stop. But as a safeguard, warn her of the consequences if there's a repeat performance. It's best if the consequences relate to the crime. Perhaps if she makes her sibling's life a misery she should be temporarily excluded from the family. You could send her to her room, or perhaps leave her behind when you next do something fun. One obvious consequence could be that she has to apologize for what she's done and perhaps do something to make her sibling feel better (for more on apologizing and making amends, see pages 200–207).

Give your aggressive child some strategies

Just as many of the strategies for dealing with irritating behaviour will help your bullied child, they'll also help if your child is being a bully. But here are some more ways you can help her stay out of trouble.

Ask her what she could do instead

Try being a LAID-BACK PARENT

Ask for solutions It's always worth asking your aggressive child what else she can do when she feels tempted to hit or hurt her sibling. If the idea comes from her, she's more likely to make it work.

- *'Instead of shouting at her and calling names, what do you think you might do next time your sister gets on your nerves?'*

If she's very strong-willed and independent, and insists on doing things her own way, give her the chance to speak up for herself and be responsible. Try asking:

- *'What could you do differently?'*

Then thank her for any helpful suggestions.

Encourage her to come and talk to you

Try being a TUNED-IN PARENT

Accept difficult feelings Make sure your child knows that she can always come to you with her grievances when she's feeling angry and frustrated about her siblings, and that you'll listen.

- *'If you're getting so furious with your brothers you feel like you want to kill them, come and find me. It's much better to tell me about it than lash out at them.'*

Like irritating behaviour (see pages 186–91), some bullying is a signal that your child has problems elsewhere, so listening should help.

- *'I heard how those boys keep picking on you. If you ever want to talk about it, let me know.'*
- *'I'm not surprised you're in a bad mood when you come home. I'm dyslexic myself, and I know how difficult and frustrating it can be. But come and talk to me instead of taking it out on your sister.'*
- *'Things haven't been easy recently, since your dad and I split up, and I know how upset you are. But it's not your brother's fault, and he's feeling as shell-shocked as you are. Instead of shouting at him, let me know when you're upset.'*

Suggest ways to work off her aggression

Try being a SORTED PARENT

Train them up Give your child suggestions about what she can do when she's tempted to hurt her sibling:

- *'If you notice you're starting to get angry, do something about it. Get well away from your brother and go and play outside. If it's too late and you already want to pull his head off, try kicking a football against the wall – you could imagine it's him.'*

If you're worried that there's a serious problem between your children, contact an anti-bullying helpline, like ChildLine, for more advice.

Saying Sorry and Making Amends

Saying sorry can be such an effective way to prevent resentment from building up. It can end little skirmishes as well as more complicated issues, and make both children feel better. If you're lucky, all you'll have to do is remind them to get on with it:

- *'Your sister didn't like being called a moronic loser and is very upset. What do you need to do about it?'*

But some parents find, however much they coax or threaten, their children won't apologize. If your children are digging in their heels, here's how you can encourage them to say sorry and make amends.

Prepare the ground

Try being a SORTED PARENT

Train them up If you have small children, you could get them into the habit of apologizing early. Every time they snatch a toy or hurt their sibling, say something like:

- *'We don't hit people on the head with building blocks. Tell Susie you're sorry.'*

It can be easy when they're little because they'll often do what you say. Once they've apologized, that's the end of it and they can get on with playing.

Try being a LAID-BACK PARENT

Be a role model Whatever their age, it helps a lot if you can set your children a good example. If you accidentally step on someone's toe or say something you regret, go ahead and apologize. You might be doing it already:

- At the supermarket or the airport, say sorry if you bump into someone with your trolley. As you know, some people don't bother.
- When you step on the dog's tail, show her you're sorry by making a fuss of her and stroking her.
- If you have a go at your children and feel bad about it, then apologize to them too.

I was packing for our holiday (not my favourite job) and one by one my children kept coming in with all sorts of stupid complaints. 'Why did you pack my pink flip-flops? You know I like the flowery ones,' and so on.

Eventually I got so annoyed that I snapped and shouted at all of them. Then they started crying and said they didn't want to go on holiday with me anyway.

Once I'd had a chance to calm down, I felt terrible about it. I realized I could have handled the situation so much better. So I said I was sorry and they said they understood how stressed I was. I felt much better after that.

Your children are much more likely to rise to the occasion if apologizing is something that's regularly done in your house. If you show them that you also make mistakes, but that you try to make things better afterwards, they'll see that it's no big deal to do the same.

Help your child work through her feelings

Try being a PAUSE PARENT

Wait until later If one of your children has done something horrendous and the others are upset about it, you might be desperate to get her to say sorry simply to put an end to the negative energy swirling around.

But if she isn't yet ready, there's no point in forcing her. If you only manage to get her to hiss an apology through gritted teeth, it isn't worth much, so there's no reason to get embroiled in a pointless discussion about it. It might be better to leave her to calm down. This doesn't mean ignoring the problem altogether or letting her get away with appalling behaviour. We're simply pointing out that she may be more amenable later.

Try being a TUNED-IN PARENT

Listen to their feelings If your child is still reluctant to apologize, it's probably because she's indignant about what happened. Here are some reasons she may be digging in her heels:

- She feels justified for what she did. If her sibling drove her to it, then why should she say sorry?

- She's feeling resentful about old grievances. She might be festering over the things her sibling's done to her in the past.

- She's irritated with you and doesn't want to do what you say. She'd rather die than give in.

- She's embarrassed and she wants to save face. It would be excruciating to admit out loud that she's in the wrong.

- She's upset with herself already. It was an accident and she'd rather not talk about it.

- She'd rather be left alone to watch TV. What's the big deal anyway? Her sibling's always moaning and so are you.

If her feelings are strong, there's no chance she'll cooperate if you don't acknowledge them. If you say:

- *'I don't want to hear any of your excuses. You had no right to hit your sister, and now she's crying. Get in there and say sorry, NOW!'*

she's likely to think:

- *'That cry-baby. She's just trying to get me into trouble. I HATE her!'*

But if you listen and show you understand her:

- *'Oh, I see. She tripped you, and that's why you thumped her back,'*

she might think:

- *'Yes. That's what happened. She shouldn't have tripped me. But maybe I did hit her a little hard.'*

Whatever the reason, she won't admit she was wrong unless you acknowledge you've heard her side of the story. So you need to tune in.

My sister and I fought a lot because she really got on my nerves. She always tried to wind me up by jumping around, butting into my conversations and trying to be the centre of attention. She'd irritate me so much I'd eventually punch her.

But my mother thought she was sweet. So whenever we fought, she took her side and tried to force me to say sorry. But she couldn't make me do it because I wasn't. My sister should have been apologizing to me.

Encourage your child to apologize

You've been aiming for that glimmer of recognition – that quiet glance down towards the carpet or that sudden look of understanding – when your child finally realizes she's been at least partially responsible for what went wrong. Now, with a little luck, she'll be more inclined to do something about it.

Try being a LAID-BACK PARENT

Ask for solutions If you've got to this place without raised voices or anger, you can again try asking your child:

- *'So what do you think you could do to resolve this?'*

You never know – she might just surprise you and do the right thing.

Try being a COMMANDO PARENT

Give information If your child can't see, or is pretending not to see, what to do next, you could give her a few suggestions. If she's upset her siblings, she needs to do something to try to make them feel better:

- *'You didn't mean to hurt your sister when you trod on her finger. But it would be nice to say sorry and give her a hug.'*
- *'Oh no, you spilt your brother's juice. If you find a cloth, you can help to mop it up and then get him some more from the fridge.'*
- *'Whoops, you knocked over her school bag. How about apologizing and picking up her homework?'*
- *'Your brother's crying. You could tell him you didn't mean it and take him for a ride on your tractor to make him feel better.'*
- *'I'm sure you didn't mean to break her hairclip. See if you can glue it together. But if that doesn't work, you could buy her another one.'*

If she feels embarrassed about saying sorry directly, you might suggest she write it instead:

- *'Sorry I kicked you.'*
- *'Sorry I touched your special pens.'*

Or if she's too young to write, she could draw a picture as a peace offering.

'I've got two children and neither of them will apologize first. How do I break the deadlock?'
If no one will make the first move, try tuning in and showing that you understand:

- 'I know you're angry because your brother called you names. And you're angry because your sister was so noisy.'

Then try being a **Laid-Back Parent** and encourage them to get on with it:

- 'If one of you would be big enough to apologize first, I'm sure the other will say sorry too.'

If one child is looking more distressed, you could also appeal to his sibling's better nature:

- 'I can see you're both upset and you've both got good reasons. But as your brother is looking a bit tearful, I wonder whether you might be really kind and be the first to end it? I think it would make him feel a lot better.'

If this doesn't work, wait and try again later, or just drop the subject. In most cases they'll come to some sort of resolution. But not necessarily – we've heard of one extreme case where neither sibling would give way.

❛ My father is an identical twin. He's a lovely man and gets on with everybody, except his brother. They haven't spoken for twenty years. They used to run a business together and one day they had a stupid argument at work.

They're just as stubborn as each other, so neither of them will make the first move and apologize. Their wives have tried to talk sense into them and so have we. But they just won't do it! ❜

'Half the time my son refuses to say sorry because he says what he did was an accident.'

Try being a COMMANDO PARENT

Give information Lots of things that go wrong between siblings aren't intentional, but they still need to say sorry or make amends. You might mention that it's actually much harder to apologize when they've done something on purpose. If they've made a genuine mistake, it should slip right off their tongue.

'Even when my son does say sorry, my daughter refuses to forgive him.'

Try being a TUNED-IN PARENT

Accept difficult feelings When one child won't accept a genuine apology, you might feel like shaking her for being so obstinate. But try to be sympathetic. Usually she isn't rejecting his advances to be annoying. Perhaps she doesn't think the apology sounds sincere enough, she doesn't want to talk about it, or she isn't yet ready to let the grievance go.

This can often happen when one child is already over-sensitized by past incidents. Even if something is an accident, she can assume the worst and insist her sibling did it on purpose. She could be right. Many 'accidents' are intentional, so she may have good reason to be suspicious.

Try being a LAID-BACK PARENT

Ask for solutions Give her some time for her feelings to subside and then ask her what he could do instead to make it up to her.

❛ My son was kicking a football and it smashed into the shelf in my daughter's room, sending her collection of glass animals crashing on to the floor. Six of them got broken and she was furious.

He tried to apologize and offered to buy her some more, but she sobbed that he'd never be able to find the right ones.

So I asked her what he could do instead. She thought about it and said he could do six favours. 'If I want a cup of tea in my bedroom,' she explained, 'you have to go and get it for me. That would count as one. Or you could help me with my homework, or walk over and turn the light on if I can't be bothered to do it.' He agreed, and that was that. ❜

'My husband says I should always make the children apologize. But I think it can be more trouble than it's worth.'

By making an unwilling child say sorry, you can cause a bigger drama than existed in the first place.

❧ *I'm so embarrassed. We went to stay with some friends, and my boys got into a fight over a cricket ball. My younger son stole it, so his brother tackled him and smashed his face into the ground. Their shouting could be heard by everyone, so I rushed out to break it up.*

I told them to say sorry, but they refused. I started pleading and begging them to apologize, and then shouting, but they still refused.

It was awful. They never did make up that weekend, and they spent the rest of it throwing each other dirty looks and shoving each other. I was so embarrassed. I ended up looking like a loser mother who can't even solve a stupid argument over a ball. ❧

If you get heavy about it, your children might end up angry with you or just decide that their biggest mistake was getting caught. Sometimes it's better just to drop the whole subject.

❧ *My children had a go at each other over I can't remember what. I asked them to say sorry, but they said they'd prefer to forget about it. I thought for a moment and decided, why not? 'All right,' I said. 'Let's do that.'* ❧

You and your partner probably don't apologize after every cross word or disagreement; lots of times it's easier just to say nothing. It's fine to let your children do the same as long as no one is nursing hurt feelings.

Encouraging Them to Be Kind to Each Other

Strengthening your children's relationship isn't just about sorting out their problems. It's also about building a family ethos where siblings appreciate and care for each other. There are all sorts of ways to encourage your children to be good siblings, and the more they see themselves this way, the kinder they're likely to be.

Try being a CHEERLEADER PARENT

Notice the good, ignore the bad One of the best ways to encourage your children to treat each other better is by being a **Cheerleader Parent**. It's so easy to notice the times our children aren't getting on, especially when they're bickering so loudly we can't hear ourselves think. But even if your children fight quite a bit, there are likely to be lots of little things they do for each other. When one of your children is actually kind to her siblings, show her you've noticed because it's the best way to encourage her to do it again. Anything complimentary you can say is wonderful. Try:

- *'I love the way you're making the baby laugh.'*
- *'You're so kind to give your brother some of your sweets.'*
- *'It was great the way you held his other hand when we were crossing the road.'*

Most children desperately want attention, and will do whatever it takes to get it. So, instead of giving them negative attention when they're rotten to their siblings, swing it round and give them lots of positive attention when they treat each other well. If you think you might get annoying by praising them all the time, try a thumbs-up, a smile or a quick nod.

Be positive While our children are young, they look to us to interpret their world. By focusing on the kind things they do for each other, you can help them see each other, and themselves, in a positive way. Here are some things you can try.

Encourage them to see each other as supportive siblings

Try passing on compliments between them. Everyone likes to be appreciated. If your children realize their siblings value them, they may start seeing each other in a new way and being nicer in return:

- *'Sam mentioned you taught him how to be a goalie. He really liked that.'*
- *'Jen says she couldn't have transferred all those songs on to her iPod without you.'*

Encourage them to say nice things about each other
When one child surprises you and says something complimentary about a sibling, be sure to comment on it.

- *'Yes – she did paint a lovely picture. Thanks for telling her you like it.'*

You might be amazed how keen younger children can be.

❝ At school, my daughter did something called Circle Time with her class. They took turns saying something positive about the person sitting next to them. She told us about it at tea and my son asked if we could try it. ❞

Encourage them to be caring and affectionate
One of the best ways to encourage your children to be affectionate is to be affectionate towards them. Perhaps you could give them a hug and a kiss when you see them in the morning, when you collect them from school and when they go to sleep at night. Or snuggle up with them to read a story or watch TV.

❝ One of my children's favourite treats is to watch a movie. We huddle up together on the sofa with a duvet. ❞

You might comment on how lovely it is to be there all together, or even take a photograph to show them how sweet they look.

Encourage them to help each other and do things together
Children often love helping each other. If you've got a baby, encourage your older children to fetch nappy cream and entertain him. As they get older, they can read books, or teach each other new tricks on the computer. And when they're older still, they can walk together to the corner shop or home from school.

Here's how one grandmother we know encourages her grand-children to look after each other.

> If David falls down, I might say to Claire, 'Oh dear. Run over and give him a hug and tell him I'll be along in a minute.' I want them to see that they can look after each other, not just compete with each other for my attention.

Encourage them to think of each other with family rituals

Most children love special celebrations, like birthdays and Christmas, and can get a lot of satisfaction from choosing each other's presents. So when their sibling's birthday is coming up, you could remind them to make a card or take them out shopping to buy gifts.

> When my children were little I'd take them out every year to shop for each other for Christmas. They LOVED it. We'd all be in the shop to-gether, and they'd each keep pulling me to the side. 'Do you think she'd like . . . ?' 'What about giving him . . . ?' Then they'd keep looking round the shop while I hid all the presents and paid for them.

It can be very useful to remember this enthusiasm, and remind them of it when they aren't getting on:

- 'I know it seems as if he hates you, but do you remember how excited he was when we were choosing your Christmas present? He was so keen to find something you'd really like.'

You can also get them involved in planning events and parties to make their sibling's day special.

> My children love organizing each other's birthday parties. They sit in bed together at night and think up all the events they'd like to do, like relay races, sucking up chocolate buttons with a straw and hanging doughnuts from a tree. They work out what games they want to play and help to fill the party bags. On the day, they also love to help run the party.

If your children get used to marking special events as a family, these can become part of the glue that binds them together in later life.

My sisters and I live on different continents, but we never forget each other's birthdays. However busy we are, we make sure we call or Skype on the day.

You could also encourage other family rituals your children can do together, like bringing adults breakfast in bed on birthdays or helping to prepare dinner on special occasions like Christmas.

Encourage them to see each other as people, not just siblings

Some siblings get pigeonholed into particular roles within their families and it can be very hard to break out of them. In some families they never do.

Even though I've got a business, a mortgage and three children, when I see my two older sisters I'm still the little tag-along who can't get anything right. Effectively we're all the same age now, but they still feel they know best about everything.

There may be a very clear pecking order now, but tell your children that as they grow up, things are going to change. The older ones won't necessarily be the tallest when they're adults, or the best at everything. Their relationship with each other is probably going to be the longest of their lives, and for most of it they're going to be adults on an equal footing. So they might as well consider that possibility now.

Building Shared Experiences

A very good way to help children build a better relationship is to make sure that they have plenty of fun together and store up happy memories. It's an upward spiral – once they get along better, you'll all look forward to spending more time as a family.

Try being a SORTED PARENT

Sort your systems **Sorted Parents** know that when children have too much time on their hands, they can pick fights just because they're bored. But when they do things together, they'll have a great time and lots to talk about.

If you have a large family, it can be fun for different combinations of children to do something special, though it doesn't have to be anything major. If one or two are away for a sleepover, you might organize something with the others, like renting a film or going out for pizza. Changes to the mix can alter the entire family dynamic, and often for the better. New allegiances can form between siblings who don't usually get on so well.

Some larger families find taking a different combination of their children on short trips can be a wonderful way for their children to bond.

❧ *My middle children weren't getting on at all, so I took just the two of them to the seaside for the weekend. We had a fantastic time. Being away, without their siblings, gave them the chance to see each other in a different way. It was an absolute turning-point in their relationship. I took lots of photographs of them together, and they look so happy. When they got home they both pinned them up in their bedrooms.* ❧

But some families find taking different combinations of children on holiday can cause a lot of jealousy and be more trouble than it's worth.

❧ *My husband and I took two of our children away for the weekend and left the other two to stay with cousins. But they were super-jealous of their siblings and still go on about how they were left behind.* ❧

Other big families find it works much better if they plan a similar outing, but on a smaller scale.

With five children of different ages, we tend to think of them as the two big ones and the three little ones. But sometimes it's really nice to shake things up a bit. For example, my husband might take the oldest and youngest to the park, while I take the others shopping. It just gives them a chance to do things with their other siblings.

Try being a PHYSICAL PARENT

Get them moving So many good times that adult siblings remember with affection are when they enjoyed sporty, outdoorsy things together, like playing in the garden or at the beach. It's when they're outside, spontaneously mucking about, that they can have the most fun.

Parents who live in a sunnier climate have an easier time, because it's so natural for their children to be outdoors.

What did my siblings and I do together in California? We cycled and played handball and basketball every afternoon. It was great!

But getting children outside and playing together when the weather's rotten isn't easy. So we started asking parents, mostly from places where the weather is worse, how they get their children out of the house.

In Norway, where there's snow for more than six months of the year, children stick on a pair of old skis and go cross-country skiing. They come home when they're hungry. In Canada, where it's equally snowy and regularly minus 20 (and gets even colder than minus 30, giving a new meaning to the word 'cold'), they go ice-skating. There are even rinks in shopping malls, so they skate while their parents run errands. In Holland, where it rains about as much as it does in the UK, children get out and cycle everywhere.

Whatever the weather, it's a question of getting your children into the habit of going outside. If you're lucky enough to have a garden, it's a lot easier because you can turf them out to play football or swingball or jump on the trampoline. If they're little you could get them a small sandpit or paddling pool, or let them make mud pies. If you haven't got a garden, you might just have to be firm about making them come out to the park to walk, cycle or feed the ducks. If the weather is terrible, take them to the local swimming pool. Once they can swim confidently, they can have fun together for hours just fooling around.

If they've been out together all afternoon, when they get home in the evening they'll be tired, hungry and full of endorphins from all the exercise. No time, energy or reason to wind up their siblings; but lots of fun over the dinner table when they tell you what they've been up to.

Try being a LAID-BACK PARENT

Allow them to do more Laid-Back **Parents** know how lovely it can be for children to spend time on their own without anyone hovering over them. When you let them get on with it, they're sure to leave a trail of mess behind them – but they may also have a great time together.

❛ *I spent years longing for my children to get on and have fun together. Finally, an amazing thing happened: instead of fighting, I could hear them playing in the sitting room and hooting with laughter. They'd taken all the blankets off the beds and draped them over the sofas and chairs, making little cubby holes and tunnels to play in. They'd also stacked the sofa cushions up high, and were climbing up and jumping off them on to pillows and duvets.*

My goodness – the mess was unbelievable! But I kept my mouth shut. I wanted them to play happily, and I'd got my wish; never mind about the state of the house or how many hours it would take to re-make the beds. ❜

When they're having a good time, it's often worth sitting back and letting them get on with it, even if they're being a bit naughty.

❛ *My boys knew full well they weren't meant to get up and play after bedtime. But when they were small, I'd sometimes hear their little feet running to each other's room at night, and lots of giggling. It wasn't a problem to let them stay up together and wear each other out. They were enjoying themselves, and I thought they'd look back on it when they were older and laugh. I was right – they've both got children of their own now, but they still remember the fun they had together running to and fro between their bedrooms.*

There are all sorts of ways you can strengthen your children's relationship, from teaching them how to communicate better to letting them play more on their own. By now you should be seeing a lot of improvements, but there may be particular areas of friction that are still causing sibling rivalry in your family. So next we'll show you how to tackle these more directly.

6

Practical Ways to Solve Specific Problems

Tackling the Situations That Commonly Cause Conflict

However good you are at dissipating jealousy and encouraging your children to get on better, there are all sorts of classic sibling problems your family may be facing. They're extremely common, and other parents almost certainly find them just as frustrating and tedious as you do. The usual culprits are:

- **Mundane events that drive siblings crazy**
  Siblings get on each other's nerves from morning until night – at meals, at bedtime, in the car and sharing a room.

- **Fairness issues and power struggles over possessions**
  When siblings think they're getting a raw deal, they'll battle to get their share of time, toys, clothes and gizmos.

- **Gross behaviour and freezing each other out**
  It's not just about fighting; some children have other ways to get at or get away from their siblings.

- **Family complications**
  Any change that disrupts the family structure can lead to sibling difficulties, including a new baby, divorce or the arrival of a step-parent.

Many of the ideas we'll give you will not only work now, but when your children are adults themselves.

- **Preventing problems in the future**
  So many siblings fight over a parent's will that we'll look at keeping your family together even when you're not around.

Mundane Events That Drive Siblings Crazy

The Big Three – Mornings, Meals and Bedtime

Day after day, it's up to us to get our children out of bed and off to school, put meals (those endless meals!) on the table and herd everyone into bed. But if these ordinary daily events are triggers for bickering – 'Muum, he snatched the last yogurt', 'Daad, she's so noisy I can't sleep!' – they can become such an ordeal. The biggest problem times are often:

- **Mornings**
When you have to get everyone off to school, fighting or complaining can be doubly stressful. With so much to do in so little time, petty grievances are the last thing you need.

- **Meals**
Ideally family meals are a good time to chat, share news and enjoy being together. But they can turn into a daily combat zone if your children keep kicking each other under the table or making nasty, niggly comments.

- **Bedtime**
The run up to bedtime can take ages, and if siblings are competing for your attention or aggravating each other, it can seem interminable. When they're already exhausted, it's so easy for them to wind each other up, and if you're exhausted too it's even harder to cope with their tears, hurt feelings or bad behaviour.

Try being a SORTED PARENT

So what can you do to make these daily events run more smoothly? Most of the parent types will help, but the **Sorted Parents** are the ones to watch. If the same problem comes up over and over, day after day, they put in the time and effort to set up a routine to take care of it. You may not like the idea, especially if you find routines restrictive and annoying, but when they work they can make all the difference.

When things are under control, you'll feel calmer and so will your children, which means fewer arguments all round. If you're not naturally organized, you might find it hard to stay one step ahead of the chaos. So here are some pointers.

Sort your systems, give advance warning and train them up

Mornings

Sorted Parents know that if everyone is running around the house in a frenzy looking for lost reading books and bits of gym kit, the atmosphere is almost bound to be stressful. So they try to organize all the things their children need ahead of time. They also realize that the same things have to happen at roughly the same times every morning, and they make sure everybody understands this.

Aiming for this level of organization might sound daunting, but it can remove endless possible layers of friction between siblings. Every item in the house has a home and everybody knows where it is. Homework is in schoolbags. Hats are name-taped and kept together with coats, scarves and gloves. So there are no excuses for faffing around, winding each other up or snatching someone else's.

Sorted Parents also make sure everybody realizes there are certain things that have to be done every morning by a certain time, like getting dressed and brushing teeth. If their children are the type to get side-tracked, they might make a list of what needs to be done when and tape it to the wall.

When you put new systems in place and make a designated home for all the paraphernalia, it works better if you tell your children in advance what changes you are going to make and train them up. Show them exactly where to hang their coats, put their schoolbags and store their trainers so that they can find them all again. Remind them a couple of times what they need to do, and then on the day the new system takes effect they'll be mentally ready for it.

Your mornings should be calmer, so your children are less likely to squabble. But even if they do get into a row, it won't be a disaster; by being reasonably sorted, you'll have built extra time into the system to deal with minor blips.

Meals

Sorted Parents also get it that that meals keep happening daily at around the same time. So unlike those of us who are perpetually caught off guard – 'Oh blast! Is it dinner time again?!' – these parents have remembered to put a chicken in the oven an hour and a half before it's time to feed everyone. They might even have thought through the week's meals, so there's no last-minute panicking and wondering what to cook.

Sorted strategies can also cut down on sibling arguments by improving the atmosphere at mealtimes. If you're rushing around crashing saucepans on the stove and chucking plates and cutlery on the table because you're stressed and short of time, your children will pick up on it and ten to one they'll start taking it out on each other.

Instead of snapping out orders when their children drag their heels, misbehave or quarrel, **Sorted Parents** also try to give their children advance warning about what behaviour they expect. If every day you find yourself yelling at your children:

- *'I told you, it's DINNERTIME. Turn off that TV, NOW!'*
- *'If you don't stop kicking her under the table, there's going to be trouble,'*

then no one's going to enjoy their meal. You'll get more co-operation and less attitude if you try telling them what you expect ahead of time. The less stress there is, the better your children will feel and the friendlier they're likely to be. So go ahead and set up some rules:

- *'When dinner is ready, the TV gets turned off straight away – no excuses. You're welcome to pause your programme or record it and finish watching it after dinner.'*
- *'From now on, there'll be no kicking or pushing each other at the table.'*

Expect to remind them a couple of times. If you can stay calm, you'll find the whole tone at the table starts to improve.

Bedtime

Sorted Parents are great at keeping bedtimes peaceful. Though they're as busy as the rest of us, they might make it a priority to set aside time to relax with their children or read them a story. They also set up rules in advance so their children know when the TV and computer get switched off, which cuts down on endless fights about it just before bedtime. When your children know they'll each get a chance for a chat or a cuddle, they're also far less likely to wind each other up to get your attention.

Sorted Parents also make sure everyone knows what's expected of them. If you have small children, you may need to talk them through all the little steps along the way, or make a list and tape it to the wall so they understand what is supposed to happen when. It's probably some combination of tidying up, bath, teeth and pyjamas, and then it's time for a story. You could even draw it in pictures for very little ones.

Once children know what they're supposed to be doing, they're much less likely to get distracted or annoy their siblings when they should be getting ready for bed. They're also less likely to disrupt their siblings' time with you or complain that you're taking too long, if they're confident they'll get their turn.

My son used to do everything he could to interrupt me when I was trying to settle his little sister to sleep. I got angry with him each time, but it didn't stop him.

Eventually I sat down and explained that the more he interrupted, the less time I'd have for him before bedtime. I told him that the best way to get a proper long story with me was to wait nicely in his own room. Now he understands this, he lets me put her to bed no problem.

Other Ways of Managing Mornings, Meals and Bedtime

'I'm actually quite organized and my children know exactly what to do. But I still have to hound them to get moving.'

Try being a LAID-BACK PARENT

Ask the family for ideas Whether it's morning stress, mealtime troubles or bedtime battles, if **Sorted Parent** strategies aren't working well for you or your family, then try being a **Laid-Back Parent**. Instead of nagging your children, try working on a solution together so that everyone begins pulling in the same direction. Here's how one mother we know did it:

Mornings used to be awful. I was trying to get the children ready for school, the house straightened and myself off to work. But it was chaos. The children would sit around being horrible to each other and it would make me so angry.

So I asked them to help me. We made a huge list of everything we needed to do each morning – not only getting ready for school, but making breakfast and clearing it up, beds tidied, teeth cleaned and all kinds of things packed up. Once they saw it in writing, they could see why I was so stressed.

My daughter suggested we do a lot of it the night before. I'd been avoiding that because I'm so tired after work, but she was right.

My older son suggested everyone use separate pegs in the hallway so their stuff wouldn't get jumbled up together. Genius! Why didn't I think of that one?

My other son wanted lots more cherry corner yogurts, because those are the ones that everyone quarrels over at breakfast.

Mornings are a thousand times better now. My children fight so much less because there's so much less to fight about. Also, by solving these problems themselves, they're keen to make them work.

'My children came up with some ideas. But their enthusiasm only lasted for a couple of days. Now we're right back to square one.'

Try being a CHEERLEADER PARENT

Praise on the spot No matter what problem they're trying to overcome, **Cheerleaders** are great at keeping their children on the right track by giving them lots of praise. The wonderful thing about telling your children what they're doing right is that it encourages them to continue doing it.

You could praise them for coming up with good ways to solve problems, which helps them feel you value their ideas. You can also praise them for following through with what you've agreed and even for arguing less:

- *'You know, it was a great idea getting the schoolbags packed up the night before. Thanks to all of you for helping me get organized. It's made the mornings so much more pleasant.'*

'You're telling me to get organized or ask my children for ideas? But I'm permanently exhausted and my house is like a bombsite.'

Try being a PAUSE PARENT

Calm down fast Don't feel bad for one minute if you're sometimes overwhelmed by the mess and chaos of family life. Being a parent can be hard going at the best of times. If you also have a baby, toddlers, children who don't sleep much, or you're juggling a job on top, there are almost certainly going to be days when it feels as though you're walking through treacle backwards.

In the big scheme of things, of course it doesn't matter if your children's school uniforms aren't labelled, or you run out of milk or they temporarily lose their pyjamas. But it does matter if you get very anxious about it, because your children will almost certainly pick up on how you feel. If they can feel the tension in the air, they may well take it out on each other. Some children bicker because they know it's a good way to get your attention when you're busy, or even because they know you'll be less able to stop them.

So if you just haven't got the time or brain-space to get to grips with the chaos, your best bet is to try to be a **Pause Parent**. If the morning routine, family mealtimes or bedtime stresses you out, try taking a few deep breaths, walk away for a minute or so to calm down, and do what you can to keep your feelings under control. This way you won't accidentally make everything worse before you've got everyone off to school or bed.

'They're still at it! I've tried everything, but they're still kicking each other under the table at dinner and jumping on each other's beds at night.'

Try being a COMMANDO PARENT

Give information and use consequences Even if everyone knows what to expect and agrees a way forward, there will inevitably be times when you'll have to be a **Commando Parent** and enforce the rules:

- *'You know the rule. Stop kicking your sister or you'll have to leave the table.'*
- *'We will be leaving for school in ten minutes, whether or not you're ready. It's not fair for your brother to be late because you two are arguing.'*

If you aren't a natural **Commando Parent**, it helps a lot to tell your children ahead of time what's expected of them. If you set it up right, it may not be as difficult as you think to enforce consequences. Then, once you've managed to do it a few times, your children will know that you mean business. Anything you can do to strengthen your relationship with them will also help because they'll be more likely to listen (see Chapter 3).

When They're Cooped Up Together – Bedroom Battles and Travelling

Sibling arguments are often at their most volcanic when children are cooped up together. Even the tiniest things can become majorly annoying – they can get on each other's nerves just by breathing, and they can't get away from each other. Two of the most obvious trouble spots can be:

- **Bedroom battles**
  Sharing a bedroom can build happy childhood memories – but not if your children hate it, or each other. If one is tidier, one likes quiet time alone, they have different sleeping patterns or either of them is bossy or territorial, they can get furious with each other day after day.

- **Travelling**
  Fighting in cars, trains and planes can be unbearable because you're trapped in with them too. At least at home you can separate them, but when travelling they're squashed together like sardines and they can drive each other and everyone around them demented.

If you find dark, wet, rainy days are also a problem, see pages 213–14, on getting your children outside, whatever the weather.

Bedroom battles

Try being a SORTED PARENT

Sort your systems There might be all sorts of different reasons why your children are moaning about sharing a room. Even if you can't give them their own space, there are things you can do to ease the strain. Each child might need his own cupboard or shelves so he has a place to put his things, and if one child is disturbing the other, you may need to set up rules.

> *I feel bad that I can't give my boys their own bedrooms, but we haven't got the space. Sometimes they really need to get away from each other. We came up with the idea of putting up a screen, like a partition between their beds. At least now they don't have to look at each other all the time.*

> *My oldest likes to stay up reading, but his brother always wants the light off. So we decided the main light has to be turned off at 8 p.m., and we bought him a clip-on book light. That solved it.*

Try being a TUNED-IN PARENT

Listen to their feelings When your children get irritated and can't block each other out, it's amazing how powerful their feelings can become. But there's a lot you can do. By far the best place to start is by listening. Being able to unburden their frustrations can do a lot to ease the tension, which might otherwise last for years.

> *My brother was born seven years after me and he had to share my bedroom. I hated him, that little cry-baby wimp, touching my stuff and annoying me all the time.*
>
> *My parents were very dismissive. They said, 'What do you expect us to do? Move house? Stop complaining.'*
>
> *I bossed him and beat him up until the moment I left home. We are in our seventies now, and our relationship still isn't good.*

Don't worry if you can't give each child his own bedroom; just listen and accept whatever they say. As long as you don't argue back or get upset yourself, you should be able to help. The conversation might go something like this:

- *'I hate him. I want my own room. He ruins EVERYTHING.'*
  'I know. Sharing isn't easy.'
- *'I can't get away from him. He follows me around. He messes up my things. At night he makes horrible snuffling sounds.'*
  'Mmm. I see.'
- *'Yesterday I was trying to read and he kept talking to me.'*
  'How annoying, when you were trying to concentrate.'

And so on.

Listening to your child may not be enough to solve every problem. After all, he's still going to have to share, and his sibling is still going to get on his nerves. But by being sympathetic, you can help him to offload his feelings.

Try being a LAID-BACK PARENT

Ask the family for ideas After you've tuned in, your children are more likely to calm down and discuss it rationally. So ask them how they can make sharing a room bearable. You might even find they come up with a peace treaty.

My younger daughter came downstairs crying, saying her sister had thrown all her clothes and toys out of their bedroom and on to the landing. Then her older sister started crying, saying she was sick of tidying because her sister was so messy and refused to help. I could see the problem, but I couldn't see how to solve it. So I told them I'd think about it and asked them to think about it too.

The next morning they were very busy in there, and then they showed me their idea. There was a wonky line of sellotape stuck to the carpet between the beds dividing up the room. They'd both decided to look after their own side and ignore the other half.

Travelling

Try being a SORTED PARENT

Sort your systems When it comes to the dreaded travelling, so much is all about getting organized and sorting things out ahead of time. Don't just jump in the car or hop on the plane and hope the trip runs smoothly. Do whatever you can ahead of time to make sure it does.

If you're going on a long journey, it helps to organize who is going to sit where and for how long, and to pack a snack bag that isn't full of sugar or E-numbers so that your children don't end up hyperactive and scrapping with each other. There are all kinds of ways to entertain children while you travel so they won't get bored, from singing in the car and playing I-Spy, to buying electronic gadgets and books on tape. The point is to anticipate the boredom ahead of time and plan what you can use as ammunition to fight it.

> *I got so tired of the bickering in the car, I finally caved in and bought them mobile phones so they can play games and music to give them something to do. I should have done it ages ago.*

Give advance warning The more you tell them what's going to happen and how you expect them to behave, the better off you're likely to be.

> *The worst was the flight when we left on holiday last year. My children quarrelled the whole time and kept kicking the seat in front. The man sitting in it turned round and had a real go at them, and at me for not putting an end to it.*
>
> *On the return flight I told them that if they were going to argue, we'd separate them and I would sit between them. They sat quietly the whole way.*

Try being a TUNED-IN PARENT

Listen to their feelings When children are cooped up together for hours, it's no surprise they can get on each other's nerves. But if they start arguing and you try to get them to shut up, you run the risk of a huge meltdown – something we'd all like to avoid on the motorway or within earshot of two hundred other passengers on a plane.

Instead, listen to their feelings and you may find that the generalized rage, indignation or whatever comes down to a few specific complaints that aren't as overwhelming as you feared. Better still, once your children feel you've listened, they're more likely to behave. So instead of hissing:

- *'For heaven's sake! I've had it with you two. Stop fighting over that armrest,'*

try:

- *'It's so annoying for both of you to have to share it.'*

If you're sympathetic, they're more likely to stop jostling over it and come up with a solution.

Try being a COMMANDO PARENT

If your children are still provoking one another beyond belief, you might try doing your best to separate them. On a plane, you can suggest they get up and walk to the loo or swap seats. It's harder in the car, but if someone keeps getting nudged or bumped, or their sibling keeps giving them smug, unpleasant looks, it *is* incredibly annoying. So tell them they've got to look straight ahead or out of the window, and not cross the invisible line between them.

Use consequences There may come a point when, despite all your efforts to defuse the situation, if they're still fighting you've got to put an end to it. They may be fed up with each other, but they can't kick each other in the car, or annoy other passengers, or give you a splitting headache. Try:

- *'I can't drive safely when you fight in the car. So I'm pulling to the side of the road and that's where we'll sit until you stop.'*
- *'If you argue so much that it annoys other passengers, I'll ask if Dad can sit with one of you at the back of the plane.'*

Fairness Issues and Power Struggles Over Possessions

But It's Not Fair! – When Siblings Think They're Getting a Raw Deal

Sometimes it's easy to be fair: if there are two biscuits and two children, you can give them one each. Nothing simpler.

But so often being fair is impossible. If there are two biscuits and three children, you don't stand a chance of giving them identical portions and they'll almost certainly moan about it if they think they've got three crumbs fewer than their siblings. No matter how hard you try, you can't always get it right and make everybody happy all the time. Just to complicate the issue, being fair doesn't mean being equal. Should your ten-year-old get the same pocket money as your twelve-year-old? Probably not. But your ten-year-old might disagree.

So much of sibling rivalry is about perceived unfairness. You might innocently think everyone's getting roughly the same deal, while your children are convinced there are gross injustices taking place.

❝ *My son's feet grew so quickly that he needed new trainers three times in one year. The others are still complaining about it.* ❞

But some of their complaints might be justified. Some children weasel their way out of doing chores. Others manipulate things so that they wangle a better deal than their siblings, perhaps more clothes on a shopping trip or more expensive birthday presents. Before you've even noticed the imbalance, they're all wound up about it.

If your children feel hard done by, try being a **Sorted Parent** and set up some systems so everyone knows what to expect. But as you simply can't treat your children identically, it's also worth being a **Tuned-In Parent** and listening to grievances to stop resentment from building up. Here's how to do it.

Try being a SORTED PARENT

Sort your systems If your children are constantly fighting about who gets more pocket money, who gets more spent on them, who keeps wriggling out of their household chores and all the rest, try alleviating as many grey areas as possible. Without some sort of system, they can keep pestering you and moaning that they never get a fair deal.

If you can pin a few of these things down, you may be able to prevent some of this trouble. When they all know what to expect, there's far less chance they'll argue about it. We'll give you some suggestions, but it honestly doesn't matter what you decide as long as it works.

Chores

Setting up a workable system for chores isn't always easy, especially when your children are different ages and capable of different things. In lots of families there's at least one child who doesn't always pull his weight, and it can become a very sore topic.

My brother's job was to take out the rubbish and he hardly ever got round to doing it. I used to do all my own jobs and empty the bin too, because the smell in the kitchen was so disgusting. I HATED him for getting away with it. Why didn't my mother force him?

In families where doing chores isn't such a big issue, you might be able to divvy them up on the spot and find your children are relatively cooperative:

- 'Alice, why don't you load the dishwasher? Ray, could you do the pots and pans, and Lizzie, could you please wipe down the table and push in the chairs?'

But if helping out around the house has become a contentious issue between them, there's no chance:

- First you get an earful of moaning.
- Then one of them slips out of the room with some sort of excuse, like needing the loo.
- The others moan, twice as loudly, that he's left intentionally to land them with the job.
- When he doesn't return you begin to wonder if they're right. So you follow him and find he's sitting on the sofa engrossed in his Gameboy.
- He comes up with some plausible excuse, such as that he did go to the loo but then forgot to come back.
- By this time his siblings have gone on strike and are baying for blood.

Sound familiar?

Try being a Sorted Parent

Give advance warning Instead of getting into a family brawl, **Sorted Parents** know the best way to get reluctant children to do chores is to tell them what's expected of them ahead of time. Long before the next meal, these parents will start by explaining to their children what they need to do and what will happen if they don't do it. Very **Sorted Parents** might even pin up a roster, with clear instructions about who is doing what and when. They'd also make clear what the consequences will be if a child mysteriously 'forgets' to help out. It saves a lot of aggro all round if the more cooperative siblings don't feel they're doing more than their fair share.

Train them up Lots of children wriggle out of their responsibilities either because they're lazy or because they know it's a good way to wind up their siblings. But some actually avoid doing chores because they don't feel confident they know how to do them. It's worth considering whether this might be the case. Try taking time to show your reluctant child exactly how to lay the table, scrape his plate, load it in the dishwasher, and how to fold and hang up towels when he's finished his bath. Some children need a lot more guidance than others.

Try being a Cheerleader Parent

Notice the good, ignore the bad If any of your children is loath to pull his weight, try giving him a bit of praise and appreciation. Look out for anything he's doing right:

- *'Thanks for putting that tissue in the bin.'*
- *'Great, you've straightened up your duvet.'*
- *'That was so kind of you to get Jim's nappy bag.'*

With luck, he'll soak up the praise and even begin to see himself as a helpful person.

Pocket Money

Pocket money can be another toughie. Some parents give everyone the same amount, others set up a system based on age or make them earn it. Some don't believe in pocket money at all and just buy their children what they need. Whatever your system, as children get older it can get more complicated, especially if you factor in gifts, clothes, train fares, cinema tickets, etc.

If pocket money has become a contentious issue at your house, it's worth turning to **Sorted Parents** yet again for advice. They're good at organizing some sort of system to manage it.

I could never remember who got what at what age, so I sat down with my children and we wrote up a contract. Every September when they go back to school, we check the contract and give them a pay rise. That way they all get the same amount in the same school year. It's worked brilliantly.

The same holds true if your children argue about who gets the best deal when you buy them presents, semi-essential items like clothes and trainers or other random purchases. Rather than leaving them to complain about it, you could try working out an agreement.

Before Christmas and birthdays, my children used to wheedle for all sorts of expensive stuff they said they wanted. That was bad enough, but they were also outraged if they felt someone else got more than they did. In the end we agreed that everyone would have the same budget – £50 each. If they want something more expensive they have to save up for it.

Try being a TUNED-IN PARENT

Listen to their feelings Some situations are intrinsically unfair and it's almost impossible to balance up the scale. If one child feels left out or resentful about it, he can end up angry at the sibling who seems to be getting a better deal. So start by tuning in:

* *'It's not fair. You spend hours watching her netball matches.'*
  'You're right. It does take a lot of time, and it would be nice if you and I did more together.'

Once you understand how he feels, you may be able to find ways to spend more time with him too. But even if this isn't possible (maybe you have a baby or disabled child), he will appreciate that you've listened.

If your child feels hard done by or whines, 'She got more than me', there's also no point telling him to stop fussing. So what can you do? Again, try tuning in to his feelings:

* *'She got more sweets from the party than I did.'*
  'You wish you had more sweets.'

You're acknowledging his wish to have more. It's astonishing how well this can work. Just recognizing how strongly he feels is often enough to satisfy him.

Luckily there are all sorts of times when it's both easy and appropriate to give him more of what he wants:

* *'She got more scrambled eggs than me.'*
  'You're hungry. Would you like more eggs?'

* *'You're always kissing the baby.'*
  'You want more hugs and kisses. Come here and I'll give you a big cuddle.'

This way you can show him that if he wants more of something, he doesn't have to complain about his sibling to get it. He can simply ask you for it.

Accept difficult feelings It isn't always easy to tune in, especially if you don't think your children have any right to complain.

❝ *My children have so much and it makes me so cross when they play the victim over the tiniest, most marginal issues – who got an extra blueberry in their muffin, who had to carry an extra fork from the table to the dishwasher.*

But if I agree with them, 'You've taken loads of dishes over to the sink already,' they stop complaining much faster. ❞

If a simple acknowledgement isn't enough, try tuning in for longer to find out why your children feel hard done by. Though you may worry that focusing on what they want will make them more selfish, the opposite is generally true. Once they feel understood, you'll often find they become less demanding.

Tuning in can help to defuse all kinds of jealousy in so many situations when you can't treat your children equally. Quite apart from fixed problems, like bedroom sizes and age differences, you'll find that circumstances change and they'll almost certainly need different things at different times. There's nothing you can do about it, but from their perspective this can seem deeply unfair and they can brood about perceived injustices.

❝ *My daughter loves riding, which is quite expensive, and her older brother kept complaining how much time and money I spent on her. Then she got jealous because I bought him a laptop for his birthday. I kept trying to explain that they were both lucky and told them to stop whingeing.*

Then I remembered being jealous when my parents bought my sister a lovely wardrobe for her bedroom. They told me to stop complaining because I had a perfectly good cupboard built into my room, but that didn't stop me being envious about it.

I didn't want my own children festering about this kind of thing for ever. So I decided I'd try to be a bit more sympathetic. ❞

'Our oldest complains constantly that her younger brother gets more than she did. But financially, things are different for us now.'

It's hard to give your children exactly the same of everything. Circumstances vary and change over time. If you get a promotion or a new job, your financial situation may improve and you may be able to afford a nicer house so younger children get their own rooms, or more exotic holidays.

It's just not fair. My little half-brother has already been to Disney World Florida. When I was his age, we were lucky if my dad rented a freezing holiday cottage in the Lake District.

Sometimes the situation is reversed. If you lose your job or get divorced, you may not be able to afford to give your younger children what your older children got at their age.

My older sister got six years at private school, but I only got a year. My dad's business folded so I had to go to the local comprehensive. I'm sure that's why she got into university and I didn't.

Try being a TUNED-IN PARENT

Listen to their feelings When your child has a point – his sibling has got more than he did – then you need to keep the lines of communication open. You can tell him what's happened and why, but you also need to listen to his feelings about it.

We aren't saying you have to agree to change things. There's no reason to spend money you can't afford at Christmas. But by listening to him, you may be able to dissipate some of his jealousy. If you don't listen and your children feel they've got a raw deal, the resentment can build up.

My oldest sister never got over the fact that our parents paid for my driving lessons and not hers. But after the others moved out, my parents had much more money and could afford to help me.

'My youngest gets her sisters' old clothes. But the way she carries on, you'd think she was Cinderella, being forced to dress in rags.'

Getting hand-me-downs can also cause a lot of resentment between siblings. So try sympathizing and accepting your child's feelings. Once you do, you'll be in a much better position to explain why it's not sensible to buy everyone brand-new clothes.

Then you might find the problem is more easily solved than you'd think. A couple of new T-shirts and a hair-slide might be enough, as long as her sisters haven't worn them first.

'I try to be fair. I really do. But often I can't work out how to do it. Then I feel guilty.'

Try being a PAUSE PARENT

Wait until later Though lots of fairness issues are relatively minor and easy to resolve, others can be so complex you can't easily see how to solve them. Don't feel bullied into making an immediate decision; just tell your children you need some time to think about it.

> My son wanted a new bike for Christmas, and he got it. But two years later he had grown so much that he passed it on to his younger sister. He said he'd like another bike, but didn't want to 'waste a whole Christmas present' on something she'd get for free.
>
> But she complained he shouldn't get a new bike for no reason when she 'just got an old boy's bike she didn't even like'.
>
> I didn't know the answer to that one and I told them so. Being honest took a lot of the heat out of the argument. Eventually they decided they'd trade in their old bikes and choose some second-hand ones.

'My children are always running to me moaning, "It's not FAIR!" How can I get them to sort more things out on their own?'

Try being a LAID-BACK PARENT

Allow them to do more Try giving your children a few pointers and a little encouragement to sort out simple fairness issues on their own.

👉 *I've shown my children the 'one cuts, one chooses' rule if they need to share something. One will divide the piece of cake, or whatever it is, as fairly as he can and the other gets to choose the first piece.* 👈

👉 *I learned something called 'Sweetening the Deal' on a business course, and now my children use it. It's about trying to make an offer attractive to both sides. For example, if both children want to use the computer, my daughter might say, 'Can I have it now for half an hour? Then to make up for letting me go first, you can have it for forty minutes?'* 👈

Ask the family for ideas If the issue is more complicated, you might have to sit down with your children and help them come up with a solution. Fairness issues are just like any other family matter: there are thousands of possible solutions and your children are likely to be more compliant if you ask for their suggestions.

👉 *My youngest used to get upset because she'd buy her older brothers lovely birthday presents, but they didn't bother to get anything for her. We talked about it, and one of the boys suggested they each contribute five pounds towards a joint present when anyone's birthday is coming up. They all agreed.* 👈

'My children have memories like elephants. They know exactly who got what and when. I go round in circles trying to make things fair.'

Try being a COMMANDO PARENT

Give information Though you might want to be a nice, kind parent, make everyone happy and show that you don't have favourites, you can't always promise to make everything equal. Parents who try often find they actually end up making life more complicated because their children are on constant alert, making sure they don't get less than anyone else.

So instead of trying to live up to impossible expectations, start by being a straightforward **Commando Parent** and explain the situation to your children. Tell them that you couldn't make everything fair even if you wanted to. So if one child feels short-changed because his pancake is smaller, explain that all pancakes are different but you will try to look after everyone the best you can.

- *'As much as I wish I could make each pancake the same size, I can't. But what I can do is try to make sure no one leaves the table hungry.'*

That's Mine! – Power Struggles Over Possessions

There may be families out there where children never fight over toys, clothes, iPod chargers, the computer or holding the TV remote control. But for the vast majority, almost anything can trigger a row. It's amazing how a toy can suddenly become so highly sought after when another sibling wants it too.

I've got three children, and I'm embarrassed to admit we've accumulated enough toys for a nursery school. Something can sit for months in the corner, but as soon as one child picks it up, the others want it. 'It's mine!' they wail, 'It's the ONLY thing I like playing with.' It's ridiculous.

It's a classic to want what someone else has, and especially when that someone is a sibling. Anything – whether it's a single biscuit, a toy or the TV remote – can seem like a prize worth fighting for. Obvious personal possessions, like the cuddly toy or mobile phone your child carries everywhere, are rarely the culprits. It's more likely to be things that are semi-communal: the set of felt-tip pens that have drifted into the kitchen, the cycles and scooters that anyone can ride, the birthday present basketball hoop or trampoline that everyone uses.

Equipment that's only used occasionally, like a tennis racquet, may start by being a personal possession and then become communal. Other things, like wellies and umbrellas, may become joint property because they happen to be conveniently located when someone needs them. Things like computers and the TV may obviously be communal, but even if you're valiantly encouraging your children to have a real life as well as a virtual one, they're likely to fight endlessly for control of them. Anything can become a problem if any one of your children gets territorial about it.

Even if your children usually get on quite well, there may be times when disputes over toys and possessions take you (and them) by surprise. You may be astonished at how strongly your children can feel.

❛ My brother and I used to play together for hours, making and painting miniature figures and then arranging them in battle scenes. It was a joint effort and we always pooled our pocket money to buy them.

But one day I had just finished painting Sir Lancelot, and my brother got jealous. 'Give him to me,' he said. 'He's mine. You may own half his body, but you used my paint. So I get him!'

He snatched it, and this red mist came over me. I was so angry I grabbed his hair and started smashing his head on the table, over and over like a ping-pong ball. My mother heard the screams and had to come running in to separate us. ❜

When one sibling wants what the other sibling's got, the results can be quite nasty.

> *My son still has a big scar over his eyebrow. When he was a toddler, he climbed on to the tricycle and his sister got jealous and pulled him off. He fell down and cut his face open. There was blood everywhere; I still feel queasy when I think about it.*

We know of some parents who get so fed up with the fighting that they actually double up and buy their children the exact same things to avoid the hassle.

> *When my children were little they shared everything, no problem, except for one cheap, pink plastic dolls' buggy. This one toy was so popular they fought over it constantly, so I bought another.*

We're not just talking about one-offs, or little things like sweets and socks. Some parents go all out and literally buy everything twice or even thrice, from games and art supplies to basket balls – anything to circumvent the arguing. Aside from the expense, though this might work in the short term it obviously isn't a permanent solution. If your children never learn to share, negotiate or deal with their feelings, the trouble will eventually flare up somewhere else.

Try being a SORTED PARENT

Sort your systems and set up rules As with conflicts over fairness, there's no one right answer to clashes over stuff and possessions. But if you have some sort of system – whatever it is – at least your children know what to expect.

Some parents encourage their children to share as much as they can. Parents who start when their children are young usually have the easiest time of it.

> *My children have always had to share because I wasn't going to buy multiple sets of everything. We put colouring pencils and Lego in boxes, so anyone can use them. Even if something is a present, it goes into the games cupboard. My children don't seem to mind. After all, it's not much fun playing Scrabble or Connect Four on your own.*

Others allow each child to have their own territory.

> *I've told my children that if they've got something they don't want anyone else to touch, they have to keep it in their bedroom. But if it's left lying around the house, it's fair game.*

Often it's a good idea to use a combined approach. You might encourage your children to share books, clothes and games, but allow them to have their own personal things that are out of bounds for the others. If they're little, these might be their special sleepy blankets or teddies; when they're older these might be their iPods, cameras and mobile phones. You might also find some practical ways to avoid unnecessary conflict.

> *I bought some sticky labels and told my children to mark the electrical stuff that belongs to them. No more pointless fights about phone chargers or iPod connectors. Hallelujah. Before the labels they were ready to kill each other.*

'My daughters fight about clothes all the time. What do I do?'

Try being a TUNED-IN PARENT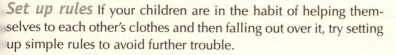

Listen to their feelings If you've got a good system going, you can bypass a lot of territorial disputes over clothes or other possessions. But you can't pre-empt them all. Don't blame yourself if you don't see an explosion coming. When it happens, listen to both sides of the story. Once everyone has calmed down, you've got a better chance of making sure it doesn't happen again. Then you can . . .

Try being a SORTED PARENT

Set up rules If your children are in the habit of helping themselves to each other's clothes and then falling out over it, try setting up simple rules to avoid further trouble.

❛ There was so much shouting and door-slamming, I told my two daughters that it had to stop. I said no one was allowed to borrow anything without asking, and no one could be pressurized into lending something if she didn't want to.

So far it seems to be working. They are being much more polite about it. ❜

Giving borrowed clothes back again, in a wearable state, is another area that may require legislation. It doesn't matter what the rules are, as long as everyone agrees to them. You could also . . .

Try being a LAID-BACK PARENT

Ask the family for ideas You could take a different approach and ask your children to solve the problem themselves.

❛ I got so sick of my girls quarrelling that I told them to come up with a solution. To my surprise, they both said they wanted a big chain and a combination lock on their wardrobes! They threaded them through the handles and now no one can get at their clothes. It's not the system I would have chosen, but they're both happy about it. ❜

'Our problem is screens. My children are always fighting over the computer, the TV and the PlayStation. What do I do?'

Wouldn't it be great to ban the computer, bin the television and vaporize the Wii, PlayStation, Gameboy, Xbox and every other bleeping, addictive, electronic machine in the house? Then our children could spend all day doing wholesome activities together, like playing hopscotch and covering things in sticky-back plastic. But it's not going to happen. In most houses the electronics are here to stay and many children find them so compelling that they will literally push their siblings out of the way to get to them. If gizmos are the cause of a lot of arguments and you're not brave enough to ban them altogether, what can you do?

Try being a SORTED PARENT

Set up rules If your children won't take turns or negotiate, set rules up for them.

> *I got so sick of the pushing and shoving over the computer that in the end I drew up a chart and gave everyone time slots every day. I know it was totally bureaucratic, but I couldn't stand the arguments any longer. It's taken the pressure off me because I don't have to be the referee any more. The chart has the answers.*

Try being a LAID-BACK PARENT

Ask the family for ideas Some parents find that their children bicker endlessly over what to watch on television. When one of them also gets hold of the remote control and changes channels without asking the others, it can lead to open warfare.

If they watch television almost every day, this is likely to be an ongoing problem, and it's a total pain if you're constantly being dragged in to settle their disputes. You could watch television with them so you can be on the spot to keep the peace, but who's got the time or inclination to watch hours of CBBC or *Hannah Montana*? Instead, try sitting down with your children and telling them they've got to come up with a system together.

> *My children used to drive each other mad, flicking channels with the remote control. In the end, after a lot of discussion, we all decided that if anyone changed channels without asking first, they'd have to hand over the remote to someone else.*

Teaching little children to share

'My children are little and they're already snatching toys from each other. How do I teach them to share?'

Sharing doesn't come naturally to young children; it's a concept that has to be learned and can take a while to sink in. It's worth remembering this if you're mortified when your toddler snatches something from another child at playgroup. Don't worry – he isn't a self-centred, spoiled brat. He just hasn't got it yet that he can't have everything the moment he wants it.

Helping your children to be patient and to share when they're small is well worth it because you can save yourself, and them, a lot of aggravation in the future. Here's how some of the parent types can help.

Try being a CHEERLEADER PARENT

Praise on the spot Little children absolutely love praise and attention, so keep your eyes open for anything that looks even vaguely like sharing and compliment them for it. For example, keep your eyes peeled for the one time your child hands his sibling a toy. If you immediately tell him how kind he is and how pleased you are, there's more chance he'll do it again. If he's sitting on the floor surrounded by a big pile of toys and he lets his sister pick one up, tell him how good he is at sharing. He'll be happy you think so, and there's much less chance he'll snatch it back.

This is all very good preparation for the times when he's the one who grabs a toy and you have to do something about it. If he already has a sense of himself as someone who is kind to his sibling and good at sharing, you're halfway there.

Try being a SORTED PARENT

Sort your systems When your children want the same toy, reassure them that they'll each get their chance to play with it.

When both of them want a particular toy, I set it up from the beginning that they have to share. 'You can play with this for five minutes, and then your sister can have it for five minutes. Then it will be your turn again.'

It works because they both know they'll get to have a go. I don't need to referee for hours because once they've had a go they usually find something else to do anyway.

Even if they can't tell the time, this system can work incredibly well. It can also help to show your children how to play co-operatively. One mother who adopted two children from China (who weren't natural siblings) did everything she could to encourage her new instant family to share and take turns.

> *I started by buying a ball and showing them how to roll it between them and play catch. First it's your turn, then his turn. There were so many opportunities to teach them to share – one had a go on the swing, then the other. One got a ride on daddy's shoulders, then the other. I tried to make it very obvious that doing it this way means everybody gets to have fun.*

'What do I do when my children snatch toys?'

If your child snatches something from his sibling, you might let him get away with it because he's only little. Or you might be afraid he'll have a tantrum if you interfere and take it off him. But if you don't step in, you can unwittingly set up a precedent that your other child soon won't appreciate. These three types of parents will help.

Try being a COMMANDO PARENT

Give information When he grabs something that's not his, act fast. Tell him nicely that he can't just snatch but will have to wait his turn. Then take the toy away from him and hand it back to the child who first had it. The trick is to be firm about it without getting angry or emotional. Then explain why you've done it:

*   '*I'm sorry, sweetheart. Jane was playing with this first and you can have a go just as soon as she's finished.*'

Try being a TUNED-IN PARENT

Listen to their feelings He's likely to be upset that he can't have the toy, so soften the blow by showing him you understand how much he wanted it.

- 'It's upsetting when you can't have what you want straight away. I know you really want to play with it.'

Try being a CHEERLEADER PARENT

Be positive If you can find something kind to say, you can help keep the mood light. If he's calm, praise him for being good at sharing and being patient. Even if he's throwing a wobbly, praise him for handing the toy back even though he didn't want to:

- 'Well done for waiting your turn.'

Then tell him something nice about the child who now has the toy. This is a clever move – it reassures the snatcher that he'll get the toy back while encouraging your other child to share.

- 'Don't worry. Jane is also very good at sharing and when she's finished with it, I'm sure she'll give it to you.'

Within a few minutes she is likely to surprise you and hand the toy over to her brother. Then you have the chance to praise her again.

- 'Well done for sharing the toy with your brother. You're very good at sharing.'

The point is to keep things moving in the right direction by telling them what they're doing right instead of getting cross or telling either of them they're selfish.

'My son keeps hogging toys.'
Just as your children need to know that they can't snatch toys, they need to know that they can't hog them either. When a child has a toy, he shouldn't be forced to hand it over just because his sibling wants it. But, on a more subtle level, children work out all too quickly the power of withholding something simply to be annoying. So how do you encourage them to do the right thing?

Try being a PAUSE PARENT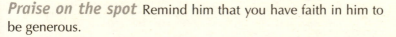

Zip your lip If no one makes a fuss, your child will probably get bored with the toy in a few minutes and start playing with something else. If you can discreetly explain this to the child who is desperate for it, she might wait more patiently.

Try being a TUNED-IN PARENT

Accept difficult feelings Then try sympathizing with the child who's hogging the toy. If he feels understood, he might start feeling more generous.

- *'It's a shame you both want the same toy, and I know how much you'd like to keep playing with it.'*

You may be relieved to find that this is enough to persuade him to hand it over. If it isn't . . .

Try being a CHEERLEADER PARENT

Praise on the spot Remind him that you have faith in him to be generous.

- *'You're very good at sharing, so I know you'll give the toy to your sister when you're finished with it.'*

Try being a SORTED PARENT

Give advance warning No luck? If you really feel he should hand it over, give him a bit of time to get used to the idea:

- *'You can play with the toy for five minutes longer, but your sister is waiting for it. So in five minutes, it's her turn to have a go.'*

Explain, too, when he can count on getting it back:

- *'Then she'll give it back to you in five minutes.'*

This usually works quite well once you've tried it a couple of times, because both children will know what to expect. They'll be confident that they'll get another turn and that you'll be fair about enforcing it.

Gross Behaviour and Freezing Each Other Out

Don't Wipe Your Bogeys on Her Hair!

Sometimes siblings do gross things to each other that they wouldn't get away with anywhere else. They'd never dream of burping in their teacher's face, or wiping bogeys on their friend's sleeve because they're too lazy to get a tissue. But siblings often take liberties, straying into unacceptable territory and treating each other this way. We're not talking about serious bullying – just the kind of disgusting manners that you'd rather not have in your house.

The reason it can be difficult to stamp out is that some children love this kind of horseplay. The more outrageous the behaviour, the funnier they think it is and the more they enjoy themselves. In some ways it's a backhanded compliment; they know that the sibling bonds are so strong that they can take these kinds of liberties and push the boundaries of the relationship.

But it can become a big problem if there's one main perpetrator who finds it funny and the others want him to stop. If he's already worked out that it's a good way to get instant attention from you as well as from his siblings, getting him to behave can be difficult.

Even if all your children think rude behaviour is hilarious, if it's got to the point where you dread having friends over or taking them out in public, the following types of parents can help.

Try being a SORTED PARENT

Bite the bullet Part of the issue for parents is recognizing that a problem exists and making a serious decision to tackle it. Don't count on this behaviour going away on its own: if any one of your children finds it entertaining, they won't be inclined to stop.

> I went over to a friend's house, a lovely, reasonable woman I've always admired, and I was appalled by her son's behaviour. He bent over, farted in his younger sister's face, and then laughed about it.
>
> I was shocked at how she handled it. All she said was, 'Come on, Ron. Let's not do that to Natalie.'
>
> That was it – I couldn't believe it. Poor Natalie! She was so upset and embarrassed. I can't understand why her mother didn't make that boy apologize and send him to his room.

Give advance warning and set up rules So much gross behaviour is attention-seeking. If you keep giving them attention for it, they'll carry on. You'll have more luck if you talk to them well away from their audience. Then they may listen to what you say and take you more seriously.

> My son used to eat like a pig, slurping and chewing with his mouth open, and his sisters squealed and complained about it. He'd keep doing it on purpose to annoy them. It annoyed me too, but I couldn't make him stop.
>
> After nagging at him for months, I decided to try talking to him in private. I explained why it bothered everyone, and told him he'd have to leave the table if it ever happened again. He finally got the message.

The key is to give your child advance warning and discuss the consequences if he does it again.

Try being a COMMANDO PARENT

Use consequences If someone's being disgusting, the rest of the family don't want them around so the logical consequence might be to send them to their room. Or if the behaviour is pretty mild, saying sorry may be enough.

When you tell your children the consequences they'll probably try it on another couple of times just to see if you're serious. But be firm, because your other children shouldn't have to keep putting up with a joke that's wearing very thin. Your child will soon get the message that you mean business.

Try being a CHEERLEADER PARENT

Notice the good, ignore the bad Try to fill up your child's attention-seeking hole with lots of praise, but only when he isn't doing something unspeakable to wind up his siblings. You could be direct about it: tell him how pleased you are when he blows his nose on a tissue instead of his sister's hair. But also, give him lots of praise for anything he does well.

- *'Thanks for helping Susannah with her reading.'*
- *'You've put away all the DVDs. Well done.'*

You could also ask him about his day, what happened at school and so on. The more attention he gets, the less likely he is to do something outrageous to get a reaction.

If the belching, farting, spitting or other gross behaviour becomes so extreme that you feel it's turning into bullying, see pages 191–200 for more advice.

Boredom

Lots of children provoke their siblings on purpose because getting a reaction is better than being bored.

Sometimes I burp really loudly at my brother just to annoy him. He says, 'Urgh, jackass, that's disgusting.' And I say, 'So are you, you loser,' and then we have a fight about it.

If you suspect the root cause of a lot of bad behaviour is boredom, try tuning in:

- *'Sounds to me as if you're trying to get his attention because you're bored.'*

Your children are less likely to go straight on to gross-behaviour autopilot if they understand why they're doing it, especially if everyone else knows why they're doing it too.

If Only They Did Fight – Encouraging Siblings to Communicate

Not all siblings bicker and fight to get each other's attention. Some of them don't talk or play much at all. As they get older and more independent, it can be hard even to get them in the same room together, and when you do, they're almost certainly more interested in texting or listening to their iPods than talking to each other. Here are some ways you can encourage your children to interact.

Have family meals and evenings together
One of the best ways to encourage your children to communicate is to make sure they regularly sit at the table for meals. There's far more opportunity to chat when they aren't grazing in front of a screen. Even once a week can make a big difference.

For us, Friday night is family night. My husband comes home early and we all have dinner. Then we do something fun, like playing cards, chess or backgammon.

Take the televisions out of their bedrooms
If your children disappear into their own bedrooms to watch TV, they might not fight, but they'll hardly see each other. Make watching a communal activity. Even if they're only hurling comments at the screen, they'll be doing something together and they'll have something to talk about afterwards. We aren't saying getting TVs out of their rooms is going to be easy . . . See pages 124–31 for ideas on getting cooperation.

Be tough on screen time
If your children have a family of Sims, 150 Facebook friends, and a whole cyberweb of internet players ready to take them on at Mario Go Kart races, who needs real live siblings? Cut screen time down and they might talk to each other. Again, to achieve this little miracle, see pages 124–31.

Get some iPod speakers for the living room
Instead of plugging themselves into a solitary world and blanking out the family with their headphones, encourage your children to share their music.

Take them out together
If your children don't interact at home, change the scene. If they're little, take them to the park or the playground. If they're older, take them skating or to the café for a frappuccino.

Zap homework
Not getting down to homework can be such a time-waster. Encourage your children to get it out of the way first thing so that they have time to do something fun together afterwards.

Family Complications

Introducing the New Baby – Getting It Right from the Beginning

If you want your baby to be welcomed with open arms by his sibling, here are some ideas that might tip the balance in the right direction.

Preparing your older child

Try being a SORTED PARENT

Give advance warning While you're pregnant, it helps a lot to talk to your child about what's going to happen. If he knows what to expect, he's less likely to be surprised, disappointed or angry when the baby is born.

It's really nice to tell him what he was like when he was a baby. All children love seeing their baby photos and hearing stories about themselves. Did you carry him in a sling? Did he cry when he wanted attention? Did he wake up hungry in the middle of the night? Did he love to hear you sing? Did he take months to learn to sit up on his own, and even longer to crawl?

Tell him ahead of time the best way to treat babies. Explain that they're quite small and delicate, so they need to be touched gently.

There's no point waiting until the baby is born and then being critical of how he treats her (see below). If you also explain that a baby can't do anything for herself, so you'll have to spend lots of time feeding her and carrying her around, it will be less of a shock when you do. You may have to explain this many times, and there are lots of good children's books about new siblings which you could read to him over and over to help him understand.

Also talk him through the practical details. If you're giving birth in hospital, explain how long you might be gone, who will look after him, and how quickly he can come and meet the baby. If you're planning a home birth, discuss with him who is going to help deliver the baby, what you might do or say during the birth and how long it might take. Let him know whether he'll be doing anything to help you, or who will be looking after him.

Nine months is a long time to wait, and the baby might seem more real to him if you show him the scan pictures and let him feel her kicking.

Try being a CHEERLEADER PARENT

Notice the good, ignore the bad Encourage your child to be kind and helpful to the baby even before she's born. If you include him in the preparations, you can give him lots of praise for helping you sort out the nursery, buy baby clothes, organize her things and choose toys for her cot. Help him begin to see himself as a friendly, benevolent sibling.

Introducing the baby

Try being a PHYSICAL PARENT

Be affectionate and just be there When you see your older child for the first time after the birth, try to make him the focus of your attention. Ask your partner or grandparents to hold the baby so you can greet him and give him a cuddle. If you've been away, he's sure to have missed you.

There will be endless times when the baby will need your lap, and your older child has no choice but to learn to share you. But just for these first few moments, try giving him as much attention as you always have.

Try being a LAID-BACK PARENT

Allow them to do more Ideally, you should be very relaxed when your older child approaches the baby for the first time. But this can be a lot harder than you think. For a start, he'll suddenly seem like a giant compared to her, and you may worry that he'll hurt her. He might stick out his index finger and poke her, or give her a big bear hug. But unless you're unlucky and his finger is heading straight for her eye or it looks as though he might truly suffocate her, just let it happen. At this stage the chances are very good that he's not trying to hurt the baby at all; he's simply touching her and getting to know her.

> *When my husband brought my son into hospital to meet his sister, we handled it so badly. Within moments, we found ourselves criticizing his every move. 'Don't do that . . . Careful how you . . . No, no, NO!'*
>
> *After five minutes we stopped and looked at each other. We both knew that if we carried on like that, we'd probably ruin their relationship.*
>
> *Instead, we let him touch her and play with her. He tried to clap her hands together, he tickled her feet and he squeezed her here and there. But they both seemed happy.*
>
> *We decided from then on only to intervene if we had to.*

Try being a CHEERLEADER PARENT

Notice the good, ignore the bad It can be hard not to be critical if you're feeling anxious, but try to stay positive.

So instead of:

- *'Careful now. Be gentle. Watch out – you're squishing her. She's just a baby,'*

try:

- *'You're giving her such a lovely cuddle. What a kind way to welcome her to the world.'*

If you've already talked to him about how babies need to be touched and held, you can add:

- *'You're touching her so gently. Well done for remembering how to do it.'*

There are so many kind things you can say, you're really spoiled for choice. So go ahead and let him know from the beginning that he's a good big brother and a valued member of the family. Try:

- *'She looks so peaceful. I think she really likes you.'*
- *'It's so kind of you to pull the blanket up for her.'*
- *'She likes the way you are holding her hand so gently.'*

Another way to draw attention to the behaviour you want to encourage is to say nice things to the baby about your older child so he can overhear you:

- *'Your big brother is so kind. He helped me pack your vests and blankets to make sure you don't get cold.'*
- *'Sam knows lots of good songs I think you're going to like.'*

Try being a SORTED PARENT

Sort your systems Take pictures of their first meeting and put them in an album. They'll both love looking back at them.

'What about giving my older child a toy from the baby when they meet as a peace offering?'

Ideally, when you introduce the two of them there won't be any other distractions from the main event. Some parents don't want to bribe their older child with presents, because this isn't what they want their children's relationship to be about.

> *I wanted my son to concentrate on meeting the baby, not be distracted by some piece of junk. What does more stuff have to do with anything?*

Some parents feel it can confuse things.

> *My daughter was very suspicious when I gave her a present 'from the baby'. She couldn't work out how he'd bought it and spent more time asking me about it than concentrating on him.*

But others want to give a gift from the baby because they feel it can help smooth the path.

> *My son carried a soft toy monkey around everywhere. I found him a miniature baby monkey and gave it to him 'from the baby'. He was so happy about it. He loved the idea that he and his monkey now had baby brothers to look after.*

If you do feel you'd like to give your older child a present, perhaps wait until after their first moments together.

'Things started out so well, but my friends and family brought so many presents for the baby that now my daughter's jealous of her.'

Try being a SORTED PARENT

Give advance warning Lots of children are absolutely fine when the baby gets gifts – they aren't interested in bootees and knitted blankets anyway. But if you start noticing signs of envy, try giving relatives and visitors a tactful warning before they arrive.

> *I couldn't believe the number of people who made a bee-line for baby Issy and just ignored Jack. Some of them also brought her fancy outfits and lovely toys. Of course she was too young to notice, but he wasn't, and he got very jealous.*

If your older child is suffering, try tipping off your visitors to say hello to him first, before cooing over the baby. You might not be able to tell them not to bring her a gift – who doesn't love the excuse to buy tiny clothes for little babies? – but ask them to be discreet about it.

I've got a large family and I couldn't stop them bringing presents for the baby. But I found it helped a lot to give my daughter the job of unwrapping them. She loved doing it.

'Oh no. I was so paranoid my toddler was going to hurt the baby that I didn't let her go near him. Is this why she's so aggressive with him now?'

If your toddler is aggressive towards your baby, there may be all sorts of reasons for it – the most obvious one being that he's a toddler. How you handled their relationship at the beginning may not even be a factor. What matters at this point is what you can do in the months and years ahead to help them get on better. We'll give you lots of ideas on handling the relationship between very young children below.

Send Her Back, Mummy! – Keeping Toddlers and Older Children Happy with a Baby in the House

For some parents the shock of having more than one child doesn't sink in until their partner has gone back to work and the relatives have gone home. Suddenly you can find you're outnumbered and coping with a tiny baby and her disgruntled sibling toddler on your own.

I thought having a baby was difficult enough the first time round, but now I feel as if I've been hit by a truck. I'm aching all over, and I can hardly open my eyes I'm so tired. Between the two of them waking up in the night, I don't think I ever get more than forty minutes of unbroken sleep.

This morning my daughter kept tugging on my arm saying, 'Play with me Mummy.' Then she had a tantrum because I was carrying the baby. I've put him in a sling so my arms are free for her, but it's making my back hurt, and I'm so tired all I feel like doing is crying.

What can you do to prevent sibling rivalry and stay (almost) human?

Try being a LAID-BACK PARENT

Get help New mothers often imagine that everyone else is coping better than they are. There are all sorts of intimidating rumours out there about women who give birth (without pain relief) and then two days later they're back on their feet, looking stunning in their size ten skinny jeans, cooking gourmet dinners or making conference calls to the office. No wonder the rest of us feel that we can't measure up. The reality is that most mothers with little children can feel exhausted, overwhelmed and sensitive for months, and need all the help they can get.

In Western countries this help can be patchy, and we often feel guilty asking for it. But in many cultures it's normal for the rest of the tribe to gather round to lend a hand. For the first month or more, women relatives might do all the cooking, cleaning and looking after older children to give the mother a chance to recover from childbirth and bond properly with the new baby. In Morocco, for example, they trace a pattern of henna on the mother's hands just before the birth and she's not allowed to do any housework for about six weeks until it's worn off naturally.

It's absolutely fine to ask your partner, relatives or neighbours to help you out, or even to pay someone else to load the washing machine, hold the baby for a few hours or entertain your toddler. If they can make your life easier, you'll feel less overwhelmed and exhausted and better able to look after your children.

If you really can't get the help you'd like, then the best thing you can do is to change your expectations. Your baby and your toddler come first, and if the house is chaotic for a while, there's no point getting stressed about it or feeling guilty.

Try being a CHEERLEADER PARENT

Be positive One of the easiest ways to keep sibling rivalry at bay is to give your older child lots of praise. You could talk to him directly, but another really nice way to do it is to say lots of nice things about him to the baby, so he can overhear you. If he feels appreciated, there's far less chance he'll get resentful.

When the baby was born, my sweet, lovely Connor was so jealous and nasty to her, I wanted to cry.

One day, when I was changing her nappy, I said, 'Connor's such a good big brother and you're so lucky to have him. It's been hard for him since you've been born because he's used to having Mummy all to himself.'

I was amazed! Immediately Connor went and got her two toys to play with. I wanted to cry again, this time for joy. I told Connor what a kind brother he was to share his toys.

After about three weeks of this, all of Connor's animosity had disappeared. He still brings toys to her and says, 'Connor kind.'

Be specific If you also praise your older child for helping you with the baby, you can make him feel grown up and important. There are lots of things he can do. He can fetch nappies, choose clothes, entertain the baby while you're busy and hold her bottle. Including your older child almost inevitably takes longer than just doing things yourself, but if you let him help you, it's something the two of you can do together and it's also a chance to give him lots of compliments.

Try being a SORTED PARENT

Sort your systems How do you divide your time fairly between two children? The simple answer is that you can't. It's almost inevitable your first-born will not only have less attention than he's used to, he'll also have less attention than the baby.

But you can soften the blow by double-tasking and entertaining both children at once. While the baby is feeding, your older child can cuddle up next to you for a chat. When she's in a sling or pushchair, you can pay attention to him. If you sit with the bigger one on the floor to play, the baby can lie next to you and watch you both, which keeps her entertained too.

Try being a COMMANDO PARENT

Give information Explain to your older child that even if you're busy with the baby, he can always let you know if he wants attention. Mention that you may not always be able to stop what you're doing, but you'll definitely spend time with him just as soon as you can. If you reassure him, he may be less demanding about it.

Try being a TUNED-IN PARENT

Accept difficult feelings However hard you try to focus on your older child, he may feel short-changed. So address his feelings directly. Even if it feels like a touchy subject, ask how he's feeling about the baby and if he wishes he could have more of your time.

If he's jealous or wants more attention, it's better to know early on than to let these feelings intensify. Psychologists say the experience of 'dethronement' can be very traumatic for older children and can lead to lots of unresolved resentment and sibling rivalry. So be as sympathetic as you can. If he says he hates the baby, listen and tell him you understand, even if it goes against all your protective instincts. It's much better for him to vent his feelings to you than to take his anger out on her.

'I'm not surprised my toddler is playing up about the baby. I feel I'm doing a rotten job. Help!'
Having another baby can be a huge shock, and nothing can really prepare you for it.

When my first one was born, I had a baby book that got me through everything. It had pages and pages of advice on nappy rash and colic and teething. I used it all the time.

After my second baby, my toddler started acting up almost immediately. I turned to my faithful book, sure that it would have the answer. The section on siblings started at the bottom of the page. 'To stop the older child getting jealous of the baby,' it said (yes, yes, I thought, frantically turning the page), 'make sure you give them a lot of time and attention.' That was it. I couldn't believe it.

I threw the book in the bin and burst into tears. How was I supposed to give her lots of attention when I also had a baby? Some days just getting myself dressed was nearly impossible.

If you're feeling utterly overwhelmed, please don't feel guilty about it. Things will get better over time, but until you get into your stride, perhaps the only thing you can do is to . . .

Try being a PAUSE PARENT

Keep things in perspective Lots of parents feel they're doing a useless job and short-changing their children. But it's worth remembering that since the human race began, children with siblings have had to share their parents.

I felt really guilty, as though I couldn't ever be a good enough parent to both of them. But I'm doing all I can, and they're fine. Once I realized how lucky they are compared to so many other children in the world, I felt a bit better about myself.

Wait until later Your baby won't be tiny for ever and if your toddler is being difficult, he will almost certainly grow out of this notoriously tricky developmental stage. If you can just manage to get through the next few months, little by little you will also feel less tired. One day, we promise, life will seem much easier.

'My oldest loved the baby at first. But that was before she started crawling and touching his things. What can I do?'

This is a very common scenario. When your older child finds that nothing is safe – his toys get knocked over, chewed or snatched – it can suddenly dawn on him that the baby is here to stay.

Try being a TUNED-IN PARENT

Accept difficult feelings It is perfectly normal for your older child to feel annoyed. So listen and be sympathetic and you can help to dissipate some of his frustrations.

Try being a SORTED PARENT

Train them up Then try some damage-limitation strategies. Show him how to set up toys on the table where the baby can't reach them. You could also show him some of the benefits of having a mobile sibling, with games they can play together, like building a tower of blocks so she can knock it down. If he feels that he's very good at entertaining her and that she likes him, he's more likely to see the baby as an ally than a rival.

'My older child doesn't seem jealous of the baby, but she's furious with me. She won't let me cuddle her, and when her dad comes home she only wants him.'

This is another common reaction from a sibling who feels displaced. He's angry, but instead of turning against the baby he's punishing you, and this can be very upsetting.

One mother told us that she felt gutted for weeks when she had another baby and her toddler wouldn't let her get him dressed or read him any stories. He kept pushing her away.

If your toddler is acting this way, don't blame him. Things have changed: he doesn't have you to himself any more, and if you're exhausted all the time you won't be as much fun either. But don't feel guilty about it – the baby needs you and you can't cut yourself in half. The good news is that it's a great opportunity for your older child to build a closer relationship with his father or grandparents. If they get the chance to read to him or take him out to the park, they'll all enjoy it. If you also keep trying to spend time with him, some of his upset feelings should start to dissipate.

Should your child turn against you, try not to take it personally.

> 6 When our children were very little they used to go through phases of preferring one of us. We used to joke that we were 'flavour of the month' and laugh about it. We found it would last for a while, then wear off. 9

If you get worked up, your child might see it as a way to get attention and wield power in the family, and it's likely to last longer.

'I thought two children were difficult, but now I've got three. The older ones seem happy about the baby, but they're scrapping endlessly with each other.'

Older children can take it out on each other if they're feeling unsettled about the new baby. This can be particularly hard to handle when you are chronically sleep-deprived. If you find you're so exhausted in the mornings that you can't stay level-headed when they bicker, and so tired at night that their winding each other up is almost unbearable, the best thing to do is to tell them how you feel.

Try being a COMMANDO PARENT

Express your feelings

> 6 After the baby was born, she woke me up so many times a night that I was an ogre to my other children. Then I'd feel guilty for shouting and for not wanting them around.
>
> So one day I tried to explain. 'Little babies wake up all night long. That's why I'm so snappy and exhausted. Please don't fight, because it makes me feel even worse.'
>
> It worked! They didn't argue so much and started asking how I was feeling every morning and how many times the baby woke me up.

As the baby got older, I got more sleep. But I'd still tell them if I was feeling particularly delicate. They'd get the picture and warn each other, 'I wouldn't do that if I were you. Mum is really grumpy today.'

It's so much better to be honest with your children. They'll pick up if there's something wrong anyway, and you don't want them to take it personally and assume that you're angry with them. Of course, in a way you are; but it's important that they know there's more to it. Once they understand why you're being so intolerant, they're far more likely to be cooperative.

Surviving Divorce and Step-families – When Families Get Complicated

In addition to the usual sibling dramas in conventional families, children of divorced families can face all sorts of extra layers of sadness, anger and frustration. There are any number of possible family permutations and custody arrangements. We could fill an entire book with stories of how family break-ups can affect siblings, but we'll concentrate on the issues thrown up by:

- *Divorce*
- *New partners*
- *Stepchildren*
- *Half-brothers and sisters*

If you split from your partner or get divorced, the fall-out can affect your children in all sorts of different ways. It's said that only bereavement has more impact, and it can change every relationship in the house. Sometimes the bond between siblings can become stronger.

When my parents split, at least I had my sisters. The three of us shuttled between them, and we helped each other stay afloat. We became very close. Thank heaven we had each other.

But for other siblings, the trauma can destabilize their relationship. They may end up arguing and fighting.

💬 *My brother, sister and I used to be very close. But when our parents divorced, they both took my dad's side, while I felt sorry for my mum. We were all very angry about it and things have never been the same between us.* 💬

Or they may become more distant or stop communicating altogether.

💬 *My parents argued for years. Then when they divorced, my mother got depressed and my father had a series of awful girlfriends. The tension in both houses was so terrible that my brother and I never wanted to be there. We couldn't discuss what was going on, because we were inarticulate pre-teen boys. Instead we retreated to our bedrooms or escaped to friends' houses. We can't discuss what happened, even now. But we can't have a normal relationship either, because we both remember how awful it was.* 💬

The thought of the potential problems can seem overwhelming, especially if you're already facing some of them. But we're going to show you lots of things you can do to help your children.

Divorce

Sibling issues are difficult to handle, but they're doubly so if children are upset and the adults in the house are also struggling. On top of everything else, suddenly there are two households instead of one, so money is often tight.

Try being a PAUSE PARENT

Keep things in perspective However hard you try to shield your children, divorce is stressful and they'll be affected in one way or another. Most parents split from their partner after they've been unhappy or angry for a long time. You might not think your children know how you feel, but they've almost certainly been picking up the signals for quite a while that something isn't right.

If your child is upset about anything (whether it's inside or outside the home), it can affect the way he behaves. The unhappy feelings have got to come out somewhere and home is the most likely place. Unfortunately for his siblings, they're in the firing line.

Lots of children have trouble with transitions, even in families that aren't coping with divorce. They can be a pain when they return from a sleepover, or when there's a change in the routine, like at the start of school holidays. Children shuttling back and forth to different homes means constant re-integration into families. Just when they're used to being in one place, they've got to pack their suitcases. Once they're settled at the other house, they have to shift again. So if your children keep scrapping after you split up, it's not a surprise; it would be stranger if they didn't react at all.

Calm down fast When your children take their feelings out on their siblings, you can, of course, intervene. But concentrate on keeping yourself calm so that you don't overreact and make things worse.

Try being a LAID-BACK PARENT

Be a role model If you're constantly arguing with your ex, it's likely your children will copy you and argue with each other too. Ideally, we'd all set a good example by being as reasonable as possible towards their other parent, but when you're getting divorced it's not easy. If you can't keep your disagreements low key, at least try not to vent your feelings when your children can overhear you.

Get help You might feel desperate to offload your bitter feelings about your ex or their new partner, but try not to criticize them in front of your children; it's not appropriate. Instead, find someone else to talk to, perhaps a friend or a counsellor, and chew through all the things that are upsetting you. If there are issues your children really need to know about, try talking to them when you're feeling more rational and less emotional.

Try being a TUNED-IN PARENT

Accept difficult feelings Your children may be angry when you get divorced and take out their feelings on you or their siblings. Or they may withdraw and become gloomy and secretive. Either way they need your support. Even if they don't want to talk about the big things, try tuning in to their smaller frustrations.

- *'I can see why you wish we hadn't moved. Especially now because it takes you longer to get to school.'*

Once you have an understanding of the underlying issues, you might be able to make things slightly better.

- *'I know it's difficult for you and your brother to come to my house every Wednesday night. Maybe I could talk to your mum about letting me spend more time with you at the weekends instead.'*

Try being a PHYSICAL PARENT

Get them moving If your children don't want to talk about their sadness or frustration (and who can blame them?), try getting them out of the house and exhausting them so that they don't take their feelings out on each other. If you can get them to move around, the extra endorphins can help to ease their stress.

Some adults, particularly sporty types, already know how good exercise can make them feel. But it's important to remember that exercise can't solve everything.

My mum is really good at listening and I can tell her anything. But my dad thinks we'll be fine if we just get out, keep busy and don't mope around. He doesn't realize throwing a stupid ball around doesn't make any difference. He thinks I'm just being sulky when I won't join in. But why should I pretend to be happy when I'm not?

Be affectionate and just be there Lots of divorced parents can get into the habit of spoiling their children to try and make them happy. Some feel guilty for what their children have had to suffer, others hope that being generous will make them more popular than the other parent.

Physical Parents realize that giving their children lots of hugs and cuddles is far better than buying them lots of stuff. With so much change, a new electronic toy isn't going to make your children feel better in the long run. But spending time with you can make them feel safe and secure. You don't even need to say anything. Just being with you can be reassuring.

Feed them well and get them to bed For the same reasons, some divorced parents spoil their children with junk food and let them stay up far too late. The kitchen cupboards might be full of chocolates and crisps, with a stash of money in the jar for trips to the ice-cream shop, and bedtimes might be constantly delayed for whatever's on TV.

Even if you're trying to be kind, if your children eat a load of rubbish and get overtired, they'll feel terrible and behave worse – especially if they also don't do any exercise. So it's no surprise if your children aren't getting along.

New Partners

If either parent finds a new partner, then of course it will affect the children. In the best cases, they get on better because their parent is happier. There may be other reasons why the arrival of a step-parent can improve sibling relationships.

When my dad disappeared off to Canada, my mother had to do two jobs to bring us up on her own. My sister and I competed all the time for her attention. When her boyfriend moved in it was actually much easier. He helped with the finances, so we got to see a lot more of her and didn't need to fight over her so much.

But when a new partner or step-parent arrives, there can be a lot more family stress, especially if the children blame them for the break-up of their parents' marriage. Even if the step-parent is blameless, many children feel ambivalent about the interloper.

We want our mum to be happy, but we DON'T like her boyfriend and we DON'T want him living in our house.

If neither sibling likes the new step-parent, it might make them closer. But if there's a lot of resentment or anxiety about the new set-up, it can make things very difficult. Lots of children refuse to listen to their step-parent or allow them to be an authority figure, so there can be a lot more aggro in the house. This may not cause sibling rivalry directly, but if there are a lot of bad feelings, every relationship in the family can be under pressure.

I can't make my dad get rid of her, but I'm never going to like her. If she tries to boss me around, there's no way I'll do what she says.

If one sibling accepts the step-parent but the other doesn't, they can easily fall out over it.

My brother is a complete idiot. Can't he see that Dad's girlfriend is just a gold-digger? If he's going to be on her side, I don't want anything to do with him either.

Bereavement

When one parent dies, siblings can become closer.

When Mum died, my oldest sister did her best to look after us. She was the one who brushed our hair and reminded us to say please and thank you. Her favourite phrase was, 'That's what Mum would have done.'

My father remarried, but my sister is still our surrogate mother. Even now, in our thirties, I know if I rang her at three in the morning complaining of a sniffle, she'd jump into the car with a box of tissues and a bottle of Night Nurse.

If parents find someone new after their partner has died, there can be complicated feelings to deal with. If these are never resolved, they can drive a wedge between siblings.

My father died when I was a teenager, and my mother remarried very quickly. My little sister accepted our new stepfather immediately, but I felt she was a traitor. How could she forget our real father, just like that? She's still very close to our stepfather, but I'm not close to any of them.

Try being a TUNED-IN PARENT

Listen to their feelings If you suspect your children are acting up because you have a new partner, your best option is to listen. Feelings have a way of festering, and it's better to tune in than risk either more arguments or your children distancing themselves.

Another good reason for listening to your children is that if there is a problem, you need to know about it. Step-parents get a lot of unfair press, but some of them really are bad news. If you worry that your children aren't confiding in you, see pages 99–100 for more advice. If you're a step-parent trying to start a relationship from scratch, you might also find this section very helpful, as it's about building a good relationship with a child.

Try being a SORTED PARENT

Give advance warning and set up rules A new partner will almost certainly have different ideas on how things should be done, but if they're not used to children or if they try to make changes immediately, there can be outright rebellion.

My stepmother was much younger than my dad, and she had absolutely no authority. It was complete chaos. She had her own ideas how we should behave, like insisting we ate everything on our plates. But we refused, so every meal was a disaster.

The best way to avoid this type of problem is to agree changes with your partner first, then give your children advance warning so they know what to expect. This way the adults will have more combined authority and there'll be less hassle for everyone.

Try being a COMMANDO PARENT

Express your feelings Being a step-parent can be a thankless job and you may hate the way your own children are so rude and ungrateful, especially if your new partner is also contributing to the family budget or helping you to look after everyone. When your children are behaving appallingly, of course you want them to stop immediately, but try expressing how you feel rather than getting angry with them.

It makes me very sad when you are so rude and offhand with Mike. I would be much happier if we could all talk to each other in a friendly way.

Stepchildren

Sibling issues can become even more convoluted if the new partner has children of their own. Stepchildren who have been brought up very differently often resent being squeezed together into an instant family. At least in a biological family you can hope that there's some sort of underlying blood-is-thicker-than-water bond, but that's not the case in a blended family.

You may have had high hopes that all your children would get along, share your happiness and build a loving, extended family. It can be such a shock and disappointment if things don't go as well as you'd wanted. When children from opposite sides of the family fall out with each other, it can also throw up all kinds of issues between you and your new partner. But there's a lot you can do to help.

There may be any number of reasons why the two sets of children aren't gelling. They may have nothing in common and annoy each other, or have too much in common and feel competitive.

What's my stepbrother like? Don't get me started. What a jerk. And what's worse, Mum says I have to be nice to him.

They may hate having to share their space and their possessions to make room for the newcomers.

Mum might want her partner to move in with us, but why should I have to share a bedroom with my sister so his poxy little daughters can have my room when they visit him?

They can be angry and resentful because members of the new family are usurping lots of their parent's time, attention and money. Depending on the custody arrangements, the new children may see more of their father or mother than they do.

It's not fair. My stepsisters live with my dad, but I only get to see him twice a month.

Or they may feel they're getting the raw end of the deal. If their step-parent is more loving or generous to their own children, they'll almost certainly notice.

My dad keeps going on about how we haven't got enough money, but that's because my stepmother spends it all on expensive stuff for her daughter.

Dealing with feelings

With some of these problems, there's little or nothing you can do on a practical level. You can't go back to the old set-up, you can't throw the new family out on the street, and if you could magically afford a house with bedrooms for everybody you would have moved already. But if you listen to your children and try to understand them, they may feel slightly better. You could sympathize, for example, and say how sorry you are that they have to share a room when they don't want to.

But once you have an understanding of the underlying issues you may even be able to help. For example, if your children are jealous because your stepchildren are around all the time, you might agree to take them out on their own so they don't always feel they have to share you.

Try being a TUNED-IN PARENT

Accept difficult feelings Stepbrothers and sisters can be unfairly demonized, but sometimes they really can be horrendous. They may be angry, or have pent-up feelings about the break-up of their own family, and may take it out on their new siblings. Or they may just have a mean streak. So make sure you listen to your own children and know what's going on.

> My stepbrother was a lot older than us, and frankly a bit of a psychopath. When I was five, he took the bulb out of my bedside lamp and said I'd get a nice surprise if I put my finger in the empty socket. Of course I got a huge electric shock, which he thought was hilarious. He also snapped a mousetrap on my brother's finger and pulled all the arms off my sister's dolls.

As with biological siblings, you're likely to find there are two sides to the story. So try tuning in to your stepchildren too. But if the behaviour is appalling and you have to put an end to it immediately, see pages 147–56.

Adopting or Fostering Children

Adopting or fostering a child who needs a home and giving your biological children another brother or sister can be a great success.

It took me many years to get pregnant before my son was born, and I couldn't have any more children naturally. In the end my husband and I decided to adopt a baby girl from an orphanage in Nepal. She is bright as a button and has adapted so well. Luckily my son took to her immediately and loves having a little sister.'

But it is worth remembering that there may not always be such a happy ending. If your biological children see their new sibling as an interloper, they won't be so welcoming. So listen to their feelings both before and after you go ahead with the plan; if they don't air their frustration or jealousy, it may not dissipate on its own. If they feel they've been short-changed by a needier child, they may be bitter rather than sympathetic towards him.

My parents were poor, but hard-working, and there were six of us children. Then their close friend died, leaving her little boy as an orphan, and they adopted him.
Oh you don't know what problems it caused! This boy had no self-control and was in constant trouble with the police. My parents spent all day, every day, just dealing with him.'

Try being a PAUSE PARENT

Zip your lip and wait until later If both sets of children keep fighting and complaining and the tension is getting to you, it won't help to get wound up and shout. You can separate them of course, but bite your tongue rather than say terrible things you'll regret. Of course you want to tell them they can't treat each other so horribly, but if you wait until everyone has calmed down, they're more likely to listen to you. For more tips, see Chapter 4 on effective ways to stop an argument, and Chapter 5 on teaching your children to problem-solve.

Setting up rules

One of the most common reasons for stress in step-families is arguments over the rules, or lack of them. When parents separate, it's hard enough for children to get used to two households with different rules; especially if step-parents are enforcing their own (see pages 273–4). With stepchildren added to the mix, it can get even more complicated. You can end up with two families co-existing, with different sets of rules for different children within the same house.

I only see my daughters at weekends and I don't want to waste any of that time arguing with them. It drives my new wife mad because she says I don't discipline them, and I know she's right. She's much stricter with her own children who live with us all the time, so they feel it's unfair too.

The more children there are, the more there is to fight about, from whose turn it is to use the computer, to who should have tidied up the bathroom. It can be even harder with children coming and going between different houses; each time they may have to re-establish the pecking order and renegotiate who can do what.

It's really annoying when my stepbrother comes round. He says he gets to use the computer whenever he wants because he's the oldest and he's doing GCSE coursework. But half the time he's just on Facebook. He's got no right to push me off it in the middle of a game.

When you need to set up rules in your new blended family, see the suggestions for problem-solving on pages 174–85. You may be able to sort out an awful lot of issues by having a group discussion with the entire family, or by talking to each child individually. They'll be used to doing different things in different ways, but in the end you may all be able to reach some kind of compromise.

Encouraging stepchildren to get on

Step-siblings don't have the years of shared memories and experiences that help children to build a good relationship. If you want your children and stepchildren to get on better, it may help to encourage them to spend time together. See pages 211–15.

❛ My children and my partner's children fought all the time. I did everything I could to find things they could do in common. But the best idea came from my daughter, who suggested theme nights.

We started with Italian night with pizza and Cornettos, then tried Mexican night with burritos and guitar music on the CD player. Then we did Fifties night, watching a DVD of Grease, and even World War Two night, where we ate Spam and watched The Dam Busters. They loved it. ❜

Try being a CHEERLEADER PARENT

Notice the good, ignore the bad One of the best ways to encourage all your children to be nicer to each other is to notice the times they're actually getting on. Go ahead and tell them how happy it makes you.

Half-brothers and sisters

When you and your partner have a child together, at last everyone is related; this baby can be the glue that binds the two sides of your blended family together.

❛ My older children think their little half-sister is so sweet. They love playing with her and helping me to look after her. They don't feel competitive because they're so much older than she is, and she's at such a completely different stage. ❜

If you're lucky and your children feel they get enough love and attention, they might not be jealous of the new baby. But you can have problems if, after the divorce, they're feeling left out or insecure.

> *Both my parents remarried and had more children, and I felt I didn't really belong to either family. I shuttled between the two; a leftover from a previous family that failed.*

> *My father moved to South Africa and my sister and I would only fly out to see him once a year. One day my little half-brother turned to me and said, 'But why do you call him Daddy, when he's not even your father?' It really upset me.*

They can also resent having to look after much younger half-brothers or sisters just because they're older.

> *When I go to my dad's at weekends, he expects me to look after my little half-brother. I have to give him a bath and wash his hair, and play pointless kindergarten games with him. My dad never bothers to thank me. He says he and my stepmother need a break. What do they expect when they've produced a little brat like that.*

Your child may really have something to complain about and the best way to find out what it is, and also to reduce jealousy, is to tune in to her feelings. It's one of the best ways to show her that you still love her and that her needs are also important to you. For practical advice on reducing sibling rivalry with a baby in the house, see pages 260–67.

Preventing Problems in the Future

All the effort you put into solving your children's sibling issues will not only help when they're young. By ensuring good behaviour patterns are in place, encouraging respect and teaching them how to solve their problems, the benefits will last throughout their lives. If you tackle resentment before it solidifies, you can create a good family culture so that everyone looks forward to seeing each other and spending time together in years to come. But one issue many parents forget to consider is the potential for a breakdown in their children's relationship once they themselves are gone.

When Siblings Fall Out Over Wills

All sorts of complicated feelings can get stirred up years later, when parents die and their grown-up children find out who's been left what in the will.

If one child doesn't think he's been given his fair share, or believes he deserves something different, he may feel snubbed by his parents or bitterly resentful towards his siblings. On the surface it may be about money and possessions, but lots of battles over wills are actually about feelings. Without their parents to arbitrate, siblings can behave very badly towards one another or play childish power games.

My parents died three years ago, but my brother refuses to sign the papers to sell their house. We're paying a fortune to lawyers to untangle the mess because he won't answer my letters or take my phone calls either.

The desire to have exactly what their sibling wants may never be more powerful.

After our mother died, I told my family that the only things I particularly wanted were a ruby ring and a bracelet. Next thing I know, my sister went through my mother's bedroom, picked out the pieces I'd asked for and kept them for herself. I'll never forgive her. How dare she!

Even siblings who are left equal shares can feel they deserve more.

Our parents left the house to both of us, fifty-fifty. The day after my mother died, my younger brother went over and took away a whole lot of pictures and furniture, and said my mother had always promised them to him.

Try being a SORTED PARENT

Sort your systems A good way to try to avoid this kind of grief with your own children is to be a **Sorted Parent** and make a proper will ahead of time. When they're older, you can make sure that they completely understand it. If possible, you can also help them to agree how to divide the random possessions that aren't specified in your will.

❝ My father told us that when he died we should take it in turns, oldest first, to go round the house and choose what we wanted, one item at a time. Then he suggested we should sell the rest and use the cash to balance everything up, so no one would feel hard done by.

It was such an obviously good and fair system. Though it was awful when he died, we did just what he said and we didn't fight once. My father always wanted us to get on when he was alive. I am so grateful to him for being so thoughtful about what would also happen after he was gone. ❞

Try being a TUNED-IN PARENT

Listen to their feelings There may be all sorts of complicated reasons why you can't leave your children equal shares in everything. Maybe one child is disabled and will always need more care, maybe the situation is complicated because there are also step- and half-children in the family who will inherit from another parent, or maybe there's just an old-fashioned tradition in your family that the bulk of family property is left to the oldest boy, or the oldest child, to keep it together. Whatever the reason, be a **Tuned-In Parent** and make sure you listen to all your children's feelings about it. If someone feels hard done by, it's worth remembering they may have a point.

❝ My parents are leaving everything – the house, all its contents and all their money – to my brother. My sister and I get nothing. It makes me so angry. What am I? A second-class citizen because I'm a girl. ❞

Even if you feel that you are dividing everything fairly, or that each of your children is getting what they want or need, it is still worth taking time to tune in. It's better to listen to them now, rather than let them fall out with their siblings. There may be more emotions under the surface than you think.

A couple of years before she died, my mother explained why she was leaving almost everything to my brother and sister. I've got a lot more than they have, a steady marriage and a good job, and they're struggling. I understood, but it still upset me. What I really wanted to hear was that she loved me as much as she loved them.

Conclusion

In this book we've shown you all sorts of ways to:

- Resolve jealousy, competitiveness and resentment and help your children feel closer to you.

- Stop your children's arguments and untangle their feelings before they get nasty.

- Help your children solve problems on their own and encourage them to be nicer to each other.

- Remove layers of tension in the house by targeting specific problems.

Your children's relationships with each other will probably be the longest in their lives, and when they get on they can be a huge source of comfort and support now and in the future. So anything you can do to improve their relationship is well worth it.

Whether you're fine-tuning minor disagreements or unravelling years of resentment, there are **Seven Simple Solutions**:

Try being a Pause Parent If your children are winding you up, stay quiet and do nothing until you can calm down. By zipping your lip, you're less likely to blurt out things you'll regret. You're also less likely to end up with one child who feels he's being treated unfairly.

Try being a Tuned-In Parent Take time to listen to their feelings. It can be hard being a sibling and, if they're feeling upset, it's comforting to know you understand. When there's a disagreement, tune in so you know both sides of the story.

Try being a Cheerleader Parent If you notice the good things your children do, they'll get on better and won't compete so much for your attention. So give them lots of compliments, but don't compare them.

Try being a Physical Parent Factor in good food, exercise and sleep. If they feel well, they'll be less sensitive, hostile or provocative towards one another.

Try being a Sorted Parent Explain ahead of time how you expect your children to behave. If you are reliable and have systems in place, your children will trust you to be impartial and are less likely to feel resentful or hard done by.

Try being a Commando Parent Be in charge. It's reassuring for your children when you're composed and you've got things under control. Siblings are happier if no one is allowed to get away with bad behaviour, and they'll treat each other better if they feel secure.

Try being a Laid-Back Parent Ask your children for ideas. It will help them feel more confident. You're working towards a time when they can solve their own arguments, which is also very useful for dealing with other people throughout their lives.

If you've already been trying some of these ideas, minor miracles may be taking place in your home. Your children should be feeling closer to you, better about themselves and they'll have less to fight about.

Once the atmosphere starts to improve, it's an upward spiral. Instead of assuming the worst about each other and overreacting, your children will get on more peacefully. When problems do crop up, they'll be easier to sort out and you'll find you even look forward to spending time together as a family.

Resources

Parenting Courses and Counselling

If you need more help to put these ideas into practice, try:

Karen and Georgia www.KarenAndGeorgia.com
We run fun, interactive parenting workshops at schools, offices and private houses. As well as Sibling Rivalry, topics include:
Seven Simple Ways to be a Better Parent
Boosting Your Child's Confidence
What to Do When your Child Says NO!
Bullying and Friendship Issues
Picky Eaters
Coping with Teenagers
We also run seminars for schoolchildren and teenagers on getting on better with their parents.

Other good courses are run by:
The Family Caring Trust www.familycaring.co.uk
The New Learning Centre www.tnlc.info
The Parent Practice www.theparentpractice.com
Parentline Plus www.parentlineplus.org.uk

Recommended Books

Seven Secrets of Successful Parenting by Karen Doherty and Georgia Coleridge (Bantam Press, 2008)
In our original book we reveal the seven simple yet powerful solutions to virtually every parenting problem. You'll find they can make your life a lot easier and your family a lot happier.

Siblings Without Rivalry by Adele Faber and Elaine Mazlish (Piccadilly Press, 1999)
A wise, compassionate book about tuning in to difficult feelings and praising your children without comparing them.

My Dearest Enemy, My Dangerous Friend by Dorothy Rowe (Routledge, 2007)
Explains why siblings can have such a huge effect on our psyche and includes the author's personal experience of sibling rivalry.

The Good Behaviour Book by Dr William Sears and Martha Sears (Thorsons, 2005)
Practical advice on minimizing sibling rivalry between small children.

New Toddler Taming by Dr Christopher Green (Vermilion, 2006)
Reassuring statistics from a paediatrician which help to keep sibling rivalry in perspective.

Acknowledgements

We particularly want to thank everyone at Transworld, our publishers. It is rare to find a group of people who are so utterly professional and hard-working, but also kind, funny and a complete pleasure to work with. Thanks especially to our editor Brenda Kimber, and Katrina Whone, Kate Samano, Brenda Updegraff, Aislinn Casey, Helen Edwards, Lisa Gordon, Sharon Gordon, Sarah Whittaker and Larry Finlay. Thank you to our wonderful agent, Caroline Michel, the godmother of both our books, and to everyone else at Peters, Fraser and Dunlop. Thank you, Deborah Swain, for creating and maintaining our website with such boundless enthusiasm.

We are eternally grateful to our husbands, children, siblings, family and friends for listening and supporting us as we wrestled with the ideas in this book. This project has been a huge journey for both of us and we could not have done it without you.

Most of all, we are indebted to a huge number of people for sharing their stories about sibling rivalry. This is such an emotive subject that we deliberately kept the anecdotes anonymous. But we thank each and every one of you for your openness and generosity.

Index

Karen Doherty lives with her husband and children, three girls and a boy, in London. She worked at NBC, and CNBC as a news journalist and producer. She has a BSc in Entrepreneurial Business from the University of Southern California, and an M.Phil. in Management from Magdalen College, Oxford. She is a spokesperson and Ambassador for UK Youth and is particularly interested in family health and relationship issues, and child development.

Georgia Coleridge is the mother of three boys and a girl. She is the Children's Book Editor of the *Daily Mail* and has been a reviewer for almost twenty years. She has worked at *You* magazine and the *Spectator* and has been a contributor to Radio 4's *Front Row*. She studied Philosophy, Politics and Economics at Oxford, and lives with her family in London.